THE CUTTING-EDGE
LEADER

THE CUTTING-EDGE
LEADER

LEARN TODAY to
LEAD TOMORROW

Pete Russo

RUPA

Published by
Rupa Publications India Pvt. Ltd 2022
7/16, Ansari Road, Daryaganj
New Delhi 110002

Sales centres:
Allahabad Bengaluru Chennai
Hyderabad Jaipur Kathmandu
Kolkata Mumbai

ISBN: 978-81-291-4574-1

First impression 2022

10 9 8 7 6 5 4 3 2 1

The moral right of the author has been asserted.

Printed in India

CONTENTS

INTRODUCTION

*In matters of style, swim with the current; in
matters of principle, stand like a rock.*

—Thomas Jefferson, Founding Father and
former U.S. President.

I was involved in an interesting conversation with old-time
college friends the other day. My buddy Michael, a newly-
appointed team leader, was complaining about the people he had
gotten as part of his team. 'People have *zero* work ethic these
days!' he complained. 'I have to micromanage everybody on my
team in order to ensure things get done, and when I do, it's
usually half-heartedly done, so I end up doing it myself.' All of
my other friends agreed, offering their own 'horror' stories from
the workplace to back up his claim. My viewpoint, however,
was very different. 'That's because you are merely *managing* your
people, not *leading* them,' I said.

This may be a bitter pill to swallow, but if you believe the
great majority (or all) of your team members are unproductive,
unmotivated, poor contributors or disinterested, it is a reflection
on you, their leader, rather than them. At the end of the day,
as a leader, your job is to join them and inspire. How are you
inspiring your team when they're not motivated? Do you notice
things more when your team does things wrong than when they
do things correctly—especially when they aren't passionate about

their work? If they tend not to contribute, do they understand how their role is important to the company's and their success? All these questions bring me to a larger point of contemplation—who exactly is the new-age, cutting-edge leader?

Are we leaders merely because we have others reporting to us or because we are in charge of a specific department? Are we leaders because we have a vision for the future that no one else seems to have yet? Is it possible that the answer is that we are only leaders when others follow? After all, how can we call ourselves leaders if, when we turn around, no one is following us or the initiatives we need their support for?

After thinking a lot, I believe that a leader today is someone who sparks in us, a desire to help. The cutting-edge leader makes you want to work for them, without shoving deadlines down your throat, threatening you with glares during business meets or yelling at you to get their job down. The cutting-edge leader is simply leading with their likeability and influence.

In our networked, matrixed, dotted-line and ever-changing organizational structures, a leader today must be a follower tomorrow—and vice versa. Therefore, we are not leaders simply because of our titles or responsibilities, nor are we leaders because we have a vision for the future. What makes us leaders is our ability to connect with others in a way that makes them want to help us and work for us.

I once received an email from a new colleague in South Korea, Jung-ho Min. Jung-ho needed information he hoped I could provide. However, before requesting the information, he must have first taken the time to learn about me, as his email began with a short, professional introduction—which then quickly turned personal. He congratulated me on my marriage (could there be a better way to get my attention and create in me a desire to help?) and then took a sentence or two to share his experience of marriage and his best wishes for me and my partner.

To say that his email struck a chord is an understatement. I forwarded it to another colleague, who had a similar, positive reaction. Together, we wondered whether his approach was a result of culture (my experience is that Asian cultures have a stronger tendency to first establish a relationship before turning to business.) We wished that this was practiced more in North America or the UK where we could at least understand the importance of doing so.

Although I had several other more pressing matters that morning, I placed Jung-ho's request at the top of my list and responded immediately. Why? Because I sensed a bond—a very real, human bond—with someone I had never met or ever spoken to! It seemed like if this new co-worker was an old friend, someone I would instinctively move to the top of my priority list! Given Jung-ho's personal tone in his email, I was confident that my response would be well received, which is why I responded to him before responding to the many others on my list that day (others who, by the way, do not always respond so warmly). The result was that my new colleague Jung-ho obtained the information and aid he needed, quicker than other old-time peers who might have made similar requests. He also established relationship equity with me so that, in the future should he need my assistance, I would be more inclined to help.

Of course, merely asking about family or important events in someone's personal life when you could care less is inauthentic and will only detract from any relationship you seek to create. Leading today is never as simple as 'just do this' or 'don't do that'. It's about making a *real* connection. This requires you to actually consider the other person: who are they? How do they like to work? What would they most appreciate (i.e., what will make their day easier and/or better?) It's about taking the time to try to comprehend another's world before operating more completely within it. This may entail sincerely inquiring about another's family, or it may entail getting right down to business (so as not to waste time when you know someone dislikes social chit-chat).

Many of us are overburdened by the demands of our job and family, and we unintentionally pass this stress on to one another. After all, it does have to go somewhere, doesn't it? However, we are merely shooting ourselves in the foot by doing so. We harm ourselves in unseen ways when we treat people badly—a chilly or harsh tone, an unnecessary CC to a colleague's superior, or ranting behind another's back rather than honouring the relationship by addressing the real discussion openly. We may be perplexed as to why we were passed over for promotion or why working with a colleague's teammates is usually a chore. Despite this, we fail to see our own role in the circumstance. If we want to make our lives easier, we just need to be friendlier, more consistent in our responses and eager to assist. That way, we create our own little organizational fanbase that would be willing to do anything for us, because our success aligns with theirs. Sweet!

You know it, people simply want to work with other people they like, sometimes selecting a likable person or company over one that actually has more qualifications or a superior product. Your friend might possess more qualifications or might be an Ivy League graduate, but you clear the interview and he doesn't. Why? Because he's a tad cocky, pretentious and doesn't quite know how to communicate his goals well whereas you're likeable, charming and humble. Think about how you behave as a consumer. Don't you buy more from salespersons when they make you feel like they genuinely want the best for you, instead of only harping about their products and services?

Essays, speeches, Ted Talks and articles on modern leadership already show you the evolution of whom a true leader is—in a world that is connected in ways we could not have imagined even 10 years ago. The workplace, too, is almost unrecognizable from what it was ten, twenty and fifty years ago. Not only have the positions requiring a leader transformed, but the actual group of individuals requiring one have dramatically changed. Women now make up a large share of the workforce in offices and businesses, but in the past, they were only allowed to work as secretaries. The modern leader is someone who devotes their time, energy and effort to growing employees, mentoring team members, and inspiring an organization, rather than setting the agenda, laying out a team's objectives and checking in frequently to verify everything is on track. Blair H. Sheppard, global leader for strategy and leadership, describes a new-age leader as the person who isn't afraid to take chances, to embrace change and to usher a team into the unknown. A contemporary leader will confidently tackle new challenges and welcome new ways of thinking. A leader's ability to listen is another important skill. Listening to each and every employee and team member is critical for a leader. The only way to comprehend the viewpoints of people at various levels of the organization is to listen. Modern leadership is ever-changing, but as these keynotes demonstrate, today's leader is transparent, inspiring and observant.

Today's leadership requires exceptional collaboration and interaction with others. Our ability to interact with people remains critical as our organizational landscapes evolve. Every interaction either strengthens or weakens a bond. When what we do deviates, it means more work for us and less supporters— those who are eager to help us and, as a result, follow us and the initiatives we want and need their support on.

The twenty-first century has been characterized by constant change and disruption at a blistering pace. During this period, the world has reached milestones never achieved before in history, which have greatly influenced the way people work and live. The dotcom boom, technological advancements (personal computer, entertainment), the development of the smartphone, the emergence of digital as a platform and the emergence of social media are just a few of the game-changing events that have occurred in a relatively short period of time. They have had a tremendous impact on how businesses and organizations operate around the world. Globalization and automation will have an impact on everyone in the coming decades. Within ten years, some analysts predict that machines will replace 30 per cent of the workforce.

All of these changes have significantly impacted the role of leaders in new organizations. Modern leaders now have the challenging task of guiding their organizations through a complex and continually shifting global economic landscape. The impact of these strategic forces is felt not only at a country level, but filtered down to industries, markets, segments and individual products and brands. A leader in modern times, then requires a proactive approach towards managing change and its impact on their company's growth.

A good example of a company that was eliminated from the marketplace due to its leadership's inability to effectively manage disruption and change was Kodak. Remember how big Kodak was back when you were a child? From your father's digital camera to your uncle's yellow camcorder, Kodak was everywhere, and so, its success seemed unbeatable. After all, it used to be the world's largest film studio. However, its leadership team failed to fully embrace the revolutionary shift from film to digital, because they were scared that digital would eat into their main business of film. Kodak was eventually thrown out of business and had to exit the market in many of its product streams due to the dramatic drop in demand for film printing during and after the digital revolution. Think of Nokia for another example. Nokia phones almost sound like relics from a pre-smartphone age that none of us remember now. The fall of Nokia was caused by the failure of its leader to accept changes in the market preference towards Android phones and of course, revolutionary Apple products.

Some Iconic Cutting-Edge Leaders We All Have Come To Admire and Love So Much Today

Jeff Bezos	You just saw this one coming, didn't you? Amazon.com continues to cut a swathe across the realm of retail, from books, groceries, clothing to electronics. Bezos has now moved into Washington, D.C., purchasing the Washington Post from the Graham family. Is he playing corporate defence—or preparing to disrupt American politics? You can never really know. That's what makes him so unpredictable and out-of-the-box. However, that doesn't mean he lacks stability. Bezos has been focused on long-term growth instead of the short-term concerns of Wall Street and says that he gets to 'work two or three years into the future, and most of [his] leadership team has the same setup'.

	Clearly, Bezos is ensuring that the team he leads shares his vision for the future and fosters the forward-thinking culture that propelled Amazon to its current position. Bezos' commitment to a customer-centric company philosophy is also critical. New products on Amazon are launched not because of competitors, but because customers genuinely need or want them.
Reed Hastings	Netflix made tremendous development in 2020 under the direction of CEO Reed Hastings, who co-founded the company in 1998 as a mail order movie rental service. Netflix has, of course, evolved into an on-demand internet streaming service over time. The company's stock tripled in 2013, and by September of that year, it had 40.4 million users.
	Some industry experts have noted that people are turning their backs on cable since they can get their favourite shows on Netflix and elsewhere on the web. 'Hastings could be the successor to [Steve] Jobs as the model in Silicon Valley for how to innovate,' said Paul Carroll of the consulting company The Devil's Advocate Group.
	Producing the famous political drama *House of Cards* cost Netflix around $60 million per season. Despite this, it only took 30 minutes for Reed Hastings, the popular streaming service's CEO, to accept the show. The speed with which Netflix gets things done is largely owing to staff having a great degree of autonomy in developing new products, with Hastings only intervening on rare occasions.

	He acknowledges that he often goes a full quarter without making a choice since he delegated authority to his employees. 'We ask employees to do what they believe is best for the firm.' Hastings continues, 'We don't offer them any more guidelines than that.' So far, his faith in his employees' capacity to make good decisions has paid off. Netflix has a market capitalization of over $150 billion, has a high employee satisfaction rating, and is well positioned to preserve its position as one of the most popular sources of entertainment for millions of people. See? For you, that's a forward-thinking leader.
Mark Zuckerberg	Life has been a whirlwind for the chairman and CEO of Facebook, Mark Zuckerberg. He famously launched the ubiquitous social media website while he was still in college and later dropped out to fully focus on its development. The site now has over one billion visitors and generated over $6 billion in revenue in 2013. Within his company, Zuckerberg has some innovative ways of generating ideas and fostering innovation. Facebook, for example, hosts 'hack-a-thons,' in which hackers work all night to create whatever they want. Furthermore, in 2013, the CEO unveiled his ground-breaking goal to bring the entire world online through the Internet.org foundation. 'The top 500 million people have far more money than the next 6 billion people put together,' Zuckerberg remarked. 'Getting everyone online… by building out the global internet,' he proposes.

Elon Musk	Love him or hate him, admit it, you *see* him and you want to *be* him. From PayPal to Tesla, Musk has had a key role in disrupting major industries, changing the game for the better. He's now brought Tesla to the crossroads of the automotive, energy, and utility industries, pledging to build the world's largest battery facility. His public demeanour has been erratic, ranging from making legally dubious remarks about potential investors to using marijuana on a podcast. His future moves will be closely scrutinized.
Bill Gates	A classic, right? His contributions go well beyond helping set off the creative destruction of the Information Age—though, that alone is a spectacular achievement. He has moved his numbers-driven approach into the not-for-profit sphere, where, along with his wife Melinda, he is triggering additional, overdue, disruptive change.
Kevin Systrom	This name might seem a little unfamiliar to you, but his creation surely has you on a chokehold. In a relatively short space of time, Instagram has gone from being a virtually unknown service to a must-have app and social networking platform. Smartphone users can't stop themselves from capturing photos and then letting the Instagram filters do their magic, changing amateur photos into something far more stylish. Kevin Systrom, the app's CEO and co-creator, began his creation in 2010. Instagram's quick growth saw it reach over

	150 million monthly users by December 2013, earning Systrom a spot on *Time* magazine's list of 30 individuals under 30 who are changing the world. In 2013, the app received new video sharing capabilities, which would undoubtedly help it grow in popularity.
Steve Jobs	I mean, can any list of modern leaders leave this name out? Steve Jobs is an archetypal twenty-first century leader in many aspects. By no means flawless in his interpersonal relations, Jobs is memorable for his capacity to spur innovation and harness it into transformational product lines. Just look at the success of Apple and their products such as the iPhone and the MacBook. You have Steve Jobs to thank for that and Tim Cook for more recent strides—but a lot of the credit must be given to Jobs, whose innovations paved the foundation for their continued domination in the smartphone market. His influence is so great, that the story of his career has become some sort of a 'business Bible' among thought leaders, authors, entrepreneurs and practitioners.
Jack Ma	By his own admission, Jack Ma, the executive chairman of the Chinese e-commerce giant Alibaba, owes his success to his teaching background. 'For a long time, I've sought to discover people who are smarter than I am.' And when you have a lot of smart people, it's my responsibility to make sure they can work together,' he says. And it was

> because of this business mindset that his exit from the company went off without a hitch. On 10 September 2019, Ma spent several years preparing Alibaba's current CEO, Daniel Zhang, to take over as chairman of the board. In a letter to shareholders, Ma also stated that the company he started is now 'based on systems of organizational excellence' and is no longer reliant on a single leader. 'What matters in life is how much we've persevered through the difficult days and blunders. If you want to be successful, learn from the failures of others, not from the success stories,' Ma emphasizes.

Realize what they all have in common? Vision, past-faced action, teamwork, innovation and out-of-the-box thinking. Although we may see them as some sort of untouchable business demi-gods today, they too were ordinary human beings just like me and you, with an extraordinary vision, passion, courage and the genuine urge to transform and create.

It goes without saying that our environment is constantly changing. Change is unpredictable in the twenty-first century, resulting in a situation where adaptive institutions (those that see change as a necessity) are the ones who will survive and compete. The twenty-first century is viewed as a century of global leadership, in which the concept of no bounds between nations, countries, ages, races and personalities must be grasped. This gives everyone the chance to be a leader and collaborate with people of various backgrounds and cultures. In today's fast-paced yet disruptive world, a cutting-edge leader with managerial skills who is proactive in addressing changes and embraces technology is required. This type is the combination of managerial and entrepreneurial leadership—the new leader isn't just an autocrat with a powerful position, but rather a businessperson, a manager and a transformer.

I

THE RE-WIRED LEADER

You have to be very nimble and very open minded. Your success is going to be very dependent on how you adapt.

—Jeremy Stoppelman, American
business executive, CEO of Yelp

For years, leadership was based upon the concept of control and fear. It was designed to be effective in the Industrial Revolution in the nineteenth century. However, we're far from that era, aren't we? So, we need to move far away from feudal leadership styles too. Emmanuel Lumonya, in his book *The Making of a Leader*, states that 'In organizations, real power and energy is generated through relationships. The patterns of relationships and the capabilities to form them are more important than tasks, functions, roles, and positions.'[1]

Roaring loudly, stomping over your colleagues and chewing them up is *ancient* in the jungle of the business world. Think about it: dinosaurs certainly had their place and power on this earth, but you won't see them leading in any modern-day pursuits, will you?

---

[1]Emmanuel Lumonya, *The Making of a Leader: Leadership at a Glance,* Blessed Hope Publishing, 2019.

People are now the central focus of business and leadership. If you want to become a strong leader, you must understand people. Influence is the approach that works in today's complex environment—whether it is a business organization, a not-for-profit or something in-between. Add flexibility, vision and determination and you have the most important characteristics of a leader.

Influence is complex. It is based upon many assets, both internal and external. You develop many of these characteristics early in your career, and then continue to enhance them. Your environment creates other assets which, although external to you, have a great deal to do with how things work. There are no cram courses that you can take to immediately create these assets or to change them. They are developed and earned day-by-day.

Flexibility refers to your desire and capacity to adapt to changing circumstances. It entails exploring alternatives to the way things have been done previously. It necessitates gathering information from several sources and selecting which is the most relevant. Its entire nature denotes change, which is the one constant that all leaders must contend with nowadays. Due to the matrix nature of most organizations, even CEOs may be team leaders, managers or even just members of teams at times. Leaders must be effective in a variety of roles, and they must continue to learn and develop new talents in order to do so.

Vision is the ability to 'see what needs to be done' given the situation, and determination is the willingness to do whatever it takes to make it happen. When you can identify and communicate what is important, establish a plan, then begin working to accomplish it. Others will follow. Having previously been successful creates a level of credibility and results in others believing in what you are doing.

Legendary executives like Bill Gates, Mary Barra, and Elon

Musk have had a direct impact on customers and marketplaces around the world through their own leadership and management skills. Though Bill Gates is most known for being the brains behind Microsoft, he stepped down from the company's board of directors in 2020 to focus on the Bill & Melinda Gates Foundation's philanthropic initiatives. The organization has also pledged more than $250 million to assist in mitigating COVID-19's consequences. On 30 May 2020, Elon Musk, the founder of SpaceX and Tesla, made history when SpaceX successfully sent astronauts into space to dock with the International Space Station and returned them safely in August. Since 2011, the Demo-2 mission was the first time astronauts were launched into orbit from American soil. Mary Barra created history when she became the first female CEO of General Motors and the first female CEO of a major automotive firm in the United States. Barra was named the second most powerful woman in business by *Forbes* magazine in 2018. She has been a strong supporter of electric vehicles and self-driving cars, and she has led GM's efforts to invest billions of dollars in alternative fuel vehicle research and development.

Because of their outstanding capacity to develop and their vision of what cutting-edge technology may be, all three have proven to be excellent leaders. These trailblazers challenged, directed and collaborated with their teams to build ground-breaking technologies in fields ranging from computer systems, smartphones to electric cars. Their company leadership skills allowed them to manage in both creative and administrative ways. This is the reality of leadership in today's culture. Is this an environment that you are comfortable in? If not, better quickly become so. You've already taken the first step by picking this book up. Good going!

Peace of mind, KFC's secret recipes and the longevity of a

modern leader in today's VUCA world are probably some of the rare things that one cannot find on Google. What exactly is VUCA, you might be wondering? It's become a trendy managerial acronym: VUCA, short for volatility, uncertainty, complexity and ambiguity, and a catch-all for 'Hey, it's crazy out there!'

Volatility

We live in a world that is always changing, becoming more unstable by the day, where major and minor changes are becoming more unpredictable and dramatic, and occurring at a faster rate. It's becoming increasingly difficult to discern the cause and effect when events unfold in unforeseen ways.

Uncertainty and Unreliability

An example of uncertainty in the business world would be a competitor launching a new product and not understanding how the markets and your customer base will respond—which could impact your own product sales. This is nothing new, but the impact of technology—which has been a huge disrupter in many industries—meant that competitors are much harder to spot. In a recently published blog looking at the changing face of leadership development, it cites disruptions seen in the taxi industry with the introduction of Uber and the impact Airbnb has had on the hotel industry. Understanding uncertain challenges, and having a strategy to reduce impact of these situations can reduce adverse effects on your own product sales.

Complexity and Chaos

I think you're a well aware of this point—remember how the COVID-19 pandemic slapped us all across our faces just when we least expected it? Not just us, this pandemic changed the way consumers purchased, economies functioned and leaders led. Our modern world is more complex than ever. What are the reasons given? What are the consequences? Problems and their consequences are more complex and difficult to comprehend. The various layers are intertwined, making it tough to acquire a clear picture of how things are connected. Decisions are reduced to a tangled web of reaction and counter-reaction, making it nearly impossible to choose the single proper path.

Ambiguity

'One size fits all' and 'best practice' have been relegated to yesterday. In today's world, it's rare for things to be completely clear or precisely determinable. Not everything is black and white—grey is also an option. The demands on modern businesses and management are more conflicting and paradoxical than ever before, putting our own values to the test. Making judgment demands courage, knowledge and a willingness to make mistakes in a world where the 'what' takes a back seat to the 'why?' and 'how?'

Take, for example, Buffalo Wild Wings, which found itself in a pickle in early 2012. The company, which is best known for its chicken wings, had a conundrum when the price and size of the wings it purchased began to exceed the menu price customers were paying. To tackle the instability, the restaurant chain had three options: raise pricing, reduce serving sizes or shift away from wings and concentrate on other menu items.

Ultimately, the company opted to adapt and change the wording of its wing servings on the menu, moving from a 6 or 12-piece order to menu items labelled as 'snack,' 'small,' 'medium' or 'large.' The change guaranteed a certain amount of chicken in weight, without naming the number of wings specifically. By all accounts, the change in wording had very little impact on customer perception or satisfaction. This Buffalo Wild Wings story is *just one* example of what it's like to do business in a VUCA world.

However, bad leaders know very well how to use the term 'VUCA' as a crutch, a way to throw off the hard work of strategy and planning—after all, you can't prepare for a VUCA world, right? Wrong. You can. The cutting-edge leader knows that well and good. Remember the Chinese saying, 'When the wind of change is blowing, some build walls while others, windmills.' Cutting-edge leaders do not stop changes—rather, they thrive in them and in turn, birth more changes.

In the VUCA world, leadership is not just leading a team in a conventional manner but means leading a team with a Vision, Understanding, Courage and Adaptability. There you go, your brand new VUCA.

The hard knocks of business over the last few years, and the complexities of the working environment have heaped new demands on the modern leaders. This new VUCA environment now necessitates broader and more novel skills than ever before. Reassurance and redirection, empowerment and solutions, emotional openness, and unwavering confidence are all things that people seek from their leaders. A few methods, such as learning to delegate, improving communication skills and swiftly gaining momentum, can help leaders achieve early success. However, modern leaders need much more than a handful of strategies—they need to understand and confront the conflicting demands of the VUCA world and adapt to the shifting business realities that require new behaviours, attitudes and skills consistently. As Satya Nadella has rightly said, 'The role of leadership today is to bring clarity in uncertain times. The more uncertain things are, the more leadership is required. There is no job description for what you are facing, no rule book... Today's leaders need to thrive in the face of this uncertainty.'

While it is true that the job of a leader in modern times has become tougher and multifaceted, for someone who wants to ace the role, they can boost their chances of sustained success by adopting the four dimensions of modern leadership that offer crucial guidelines for preparing and surmounting the challenges inherent in today's leadership roles.

What Are the Traits of the Cutting-Edge VUCA Leader?

- **Vision:** Theodore Hesburgh, President of the University of Notre Dame believes that 'The very essence of leadership is that you have to have a vision. It's got to be a vision you articulate clearly and forcefully on every occasion.'

    Leadership, at its simplest, is about painting a vision of the future and persuading others to follow you there. It's a cliché to say that the pace of change has never been faster, but it's true. And it's not just the speed but the complexity that is challenging for leaders. This creates doubt for investors and fear for employees—which means that the leader who can articulate a clear vision of the future for their organization and sell it to customers has never been more important. Shareholders and employees alike are searching for leaders that can simplify and clarify their world.

    Elon Musk, for example, is a master at this. He may not have started Tesla, but from the moment he invested, he presented a picture of a future without gasoline that has enthralled ardent fans and motivated employees. A visionary leader may enthral his or her employees, elicit loyalty from customers, and instil faith in investors. It's a necessary talent.

It is a demonstrated motivator for people when leaders walk their talk. Employees flock to executives that share a clear vision, often opting to work for the company over other possibilities.

To a cutting-edge leader, employees are not just processing wireless devices to make money for the company owners, but rather, multiple forces coming together to create a pool of new ideas, goals and creativity. Can a shared leadership vision get any more powerful than this?

- **Understanding:** Letting go of perceived pressure to react in the right way and do the right thing will be key here—there are no right or wrong answers. The 'be kind' emphasis is helpful, and being kind to yourself must be the starting point. More than ever, the idea of creating a positive 'Emotional Bank Balance' with colleagues is needed. Paying attention to what's going on in the lives of our co-workers and sharing your own views and tales can help you establish a strong Emotional Bank account. Making a withdrawal from this account when big adjustments are required is critical for leaders who have invested.

  It can be easy to overlook the need to continue to invest in relationships right now, and how we show that we care as leaders will look different for different people and situations. For some, it might be through providing them much greater autonomy to get on and do their job without close oversight and management. For others, it may be through extra support measures and access to resources. Demonstrating you recognize that various individuals require different things from you as a leader and that you can 'tailor' your approach to meet their needs is a crucial trait.

Also, a cutting-edge leader will also understand patterns: they assess the outcomes of their plans, decisions and past occurrences to be well-prepared for the future. That way, they are able to focus on what could realistically be done better in the future, rather than what could have been done in the past. A cutting-edge leader keeps an eye on the past to learn things and, in the future, to implement those learnings.

• **Courage, Communication and Collaboration:** Change is a constant in life, but in the modern world, it seems to happen with greater speed and be less predictable.

People do not generally react well to change because we fear the unknown; and change, by definition, represents an unknown. But, as Darwin said, success comes to those who are not the strongest but the most responsive to change.

This trait is two-fold: firstly, it is about accepting change as a constant and avoiding rejecting and fighting change out of bias or fear. Secondly, it is about avoiding bias towards existing solutions just because they are more tangible than new ideas. The cutting-edge leader showcases courage in times of crisis and communicates this bravery to their entire team.

Also, how can we forget collaboration? After all, leaders are human beings too. They cannot really be the most courageous amidst crisis and chaos without their comrades. Modern leadership doesn't mean leading peers; rather, it is all about encouraging peers to achieve defined goals, improve their capabilities, learning from each other and make them leaders for the coming generations. That way, each peer makes the best out of their specific capabilities and keeps an eye out for one another.

- **Agility and Adaptability:** One of the essential leadership skills for every successful leader is the ability to be fearlessly agile. 'To be agile' means to be able to think, understand and move quickly. When a prospective client has a different vision for your partnership, when your HR team approaches you with an unforeseen problem or even when you get a call from the high school principal that says, 'we need to talk,' being able to think clearly, assess a situation and find solutions on your feet will likely make the difference in your level of success.

  One of the ways to stay flexible in our ability to lead is by being clear on the principles that drive your decisions. Are you committed to not spending money on a new operating system or are you committed to productivity? Are you clinging to the ways you bill a client or in adding value to all of your interactions? When we are focused on guiding principles, then we can be comfortable altering our practices while still remaining authentic to our purpose.

Psychologist Carol Dweck, in her work on 'Growth Mindset', talks about the importance of failure as a route to success, believing that the word FAIL equals 'First Attempt in Learning.'[2] However, that also means being comfortable with making mistakes along the way and avoiding any kind of blame culture. The best leaders in this situation will be those who admit they don't know everything, admit their own mistakes and encourage mistakes in others. The cutting-edge leader will encourage innovation, continuous growth and shared learning.

---

[2]Carol Dweck, 'Developing a Growth Mindset with Carol Dweck' [video], YouTube, 10 October 2014, https://www.youtube.com/watch?v=hiiEeMN7vbQ, Accessed on 28 February 2022.

Ask yourself—what have I learned about myself, my team and my stakeholders that will make me a better leader?

Networking

As everyone should know, your network is your net worth. Due to the explosive growth in knowledge, you just cannot know everything. One remedy can be a well-functioning network. If I have only a limited knowledge of my own but know which people in my social environment can give me more knowledge, that is very helpful. It's not what you know, it's *whom* you know.

For example, the German company Bosch, has launched its own 'internal Facebook' called 'Bosch Connect,' which is enjoying growing popularity among employees. The company has also organized a so-called 'lunch roulette.' Every employee who wishes to participate enters their name in a raffle and is assigned a 'lunch date' from a different department and hierarchical level at random. Although this lunch date occurs only once and lasts about 30 minutes, research has shown that it significantly improves communication and overall teamwork. Isn't it amusing?

A modern company leader is already aware of the importance of informal networks. These networks probably helped the leader get to his/her current leadership position in the first place.

Sharing Is Caring

Old-school leadership packs the power of the CEO and turns employees into passive consumers of orders. As a result, the organization is only as intelligent as the boss, who alone makes all the decisions 'from above'. We don't do that here.

The new-age leader empowers by letting everyone make decisions. The organizational chart is (mentally) turned by its head in modern companies. This puts the employees right at the top. Everyone gets more power and a certain freedom of choice; this trick makes use of the intelligence and knowledge of all employees. As a result, the decision-making is more flexible and faster and all the team members feel equally involved in the success of a project.

Kill the Feudal Leader in You (Because Old-School Isn't So Cool)

Early in my career, I worked for my boss Kyle who clearly embodied a 'feudal' management style. He was blusterous and would be intentionally intimidating. Kyle was also a terrible listener, would always interrupt and would yell frequently in an attempt to get desired action and results.

Initially, it was exciting to be around him and, in some strange way, I found him inspiring. When I was in his presence, there was a certain amount of intoxicating energy, and my want to please and win his favour was strong. However, after a few months of being around him, his old-school management approach became—well, old. As I began to feel burnt out, my desire to please and excel decreased. I found myself seeking for an exit door, which I quickly discovered. It's the type of leadership where when the boss says, 'Jump', employees ask, 'How high?' The greatest approach to obtain results is to yell, bark instructions and pound fists (sometimes literally). Opinions that differ from the leader's are immediately muted, because there can only be one proper method, which is whatever the old-school leader believes.

My friend Kelly described her old-school manager through strong words, 'My manager is a bully who chews people up and spits them out. He regularly engages in verbal and mental abuse.'

She rolled her eyes and sighed wearily. 'His style is command and control, and he is not open to any ideas or suggestions. He has squashed my creativity and made my daily job a drudgery.' I pitied Kelly, but I pitied her leaders *a lot more*—they were losing out on a brilliant employee like her.

Most people, on being asked about their company's leaders and bosses, use words like 'sociopath', 'autocratic', 'control-freak', 'narcissistic' or 'mini-dictator'. Unfortunately, despite our cutting-edge world, most of us haven't had access to a cutting-edge next-gen leader. Instead of adjectives like 'collaborative', 'caring' and 'intuitive', you'll often see phrases like 'highly competitive', 'independent thinker' and 'career fast-track' in job adverts for management/leadership roles. The second list emphasizes individualism and competition, which align well with old-school management styles. You may gain temporary power by being feudal, but you sure as hell don't want to be this kind of leader if you desire long-term success in the modern world. What exactly does the old-school leader do?

- **Military-Man Martin:** Do what the leader says, and everything works. Simple, right? But not so relevant anymore.

  A lower-level employee, Chen comes to Martin with a problem and a solution for it. Martin cuts Chen off and tells him to do *exactly* what he has been told to. Why? Because Chen has much less education and fewer credentials, and so, he doesn't see the 'big picture'. What can Chen possibly contribute? He just needs to do his job and let Martin handle the hard stuff, right? *Wrong.*

  The problem of using this approach in a business setting is that your employees have a lot more expertise than a typical military recruit compared to their leaders. Admit it and accept it: you need your employees as much as they need you, because you cannot be a specialist in all areas.

If your customers or clients complain about your product or service, who hears those complaints? Not the leaders. The product quality and service complaints come to the lower-level workers. Those same workers, and the ones on their teams, are the ones who will see the problematic areas first. Given time, they will also start seeing solutions. But if there's no way they get to express those solutions, they'll either get forgotten, lost or ignored.

Your team members will feel little loyalty or ownership if you take this strategy. Everything becomes reliant on the leader. New ideas, new initiatives, product changes, vision and internal processes (including HR)—the culture you'll develop around these things will be one in which people wait (and possibly grumble) for the leaders to alter things that aren't functioning. It's not a work environment that builds trust, collaboration or teamwork. And it misses out on valuable insights and contributions that leaders often can't see. Today, talented people may flee such leaders. Others may stay and slowly become cogs in the system. If you want to surround yourself with talented people who can help you thrive, you may need to avoid being a military-man Martin.

- **Cash-Cow Carl:** Cash-cow Carl sees financial incentives as a prime source of motivation for all employees. Money talks, right? Give people more money, and they'll do anything you want. He tells his employees they will be given extra money for staying up late during the night to complete deadlines and turning up for work during the weekends. He favours those employees who do anything he wants and stay passive in return for some good old money.

The cutting-edge leader, however, realizes that money alone doesn't drive and inspire people to give their best.

It's safe to assume that many people nowadays, particularly millennials, are driven by a sense of purpose. They might want more than just a well-paying job close to home. People, at their core, desire to know that their actions have an impact on their community, society or the globe at large. Working for a corporation just to enhance the bottom line may not be a draw for the brightest minds or the most brilliant employees.

Furthermore, today's workers may value recognition and acclaim for their services over monetary compensation. Rewards such as prolonged parental leave, bringing their dog to work and flexible hours may appeal to them. They value even choosing the devices they use to do their work. To move away from being a cash-cow Carl, ask yourself:

- Do I promote the values of my company?
- Do I give people anything to think about?
- Do I demonstrate to current and potential employees how their work benefits the greater good?
- Do I provide employees with up-to-date incentives?
- All of these factors could be crucial in attracting the greatest employees to assist you triumph in the industry.

- **Result-Hungry Ron:** Result-hungry Ron doesn't care if his employees are giving their best, experimenting with new ideas or are on the verge of a new breakthrough that could change the face of his company. 'Where are my results?' he yells instead, always obsessing over facts, figures and percentages. Result-hungry Ron wants no risks or creativity, he only wants consistent results *anyhow*.

  This would be like a football coach demanding more touchdowns but then asking all his receivers to catch the ball the exact same way every time.

Sometimes, the situation demands improvisation or creativity. Sometimes, a player might have to jump. Sometimes, there will be someone in the way. Sometimes, it's just a plain bad throw. Don't get me wrong, being result-driven is fine. But results must be attainable. Attaining desired results becomes harder when employees feel boxed-in and restricted; when it's more about the role and 'whose job is that?' rather than motivating everyone to chase after the same goal and doing whatever it takes to achieve it.

If everyone is afraid of making mistakes or worried about who will get credit for a good idea, these are signs your company is being led using this kind of leadership. You don't want employees competing with each other. You want them pursuing specific goals as a team, achieving them, feeling great about it and being told so, and then moving on to the next one.

A more open, team-building and strength-utilizing approach is the one that believes good ideas can come from anywhere, and that we need to create systems and processes that will bring them to the surface—frequently.

- **Power-Maniac Paul:** Early in my career, I had an encounter with a senior leader named Paul that left such a vivid impression on me that I can still remember it like it was yesterday. It was our first meeting as manager-employee. We were less than five minutes into our conversation when Paul abruptly and sharply interrupted, 'Wait, is your chair higher than mine?' At which point all conversation was halted until we swapped chairs with one another because, as per Paul, 'employees never sit higher than their employer.'

I kid you not, this *actually* happened.

Power-maniacs tend to think they are superior to

others and have better ideas, possessing a unique insight to solve problems. They generally believe they deserve special treatment or are above the social conventions or rules. They are absolute bullies and may take credit for others' achievements or claim they know more than their peers. They are more likely to blame others for their mistakes and are less likely to apologize. 'They are hypervigilant about threats to their ego…so that any lack of admiration or criticism provokes them,' says Stanford Graduate School of Business's Charles O'Reilly and University of California's Jennifer Chatman.[3] This is commonly expressed through hostility and aggression, as you can see in power-maniac Paul's case.

Having an old-school, feudal dictator as a superior threatens employees' sense of belonging, causing a wide-range of harmful consequences. Your team members would end up avoiding discretionary work behaviours, such as helping a co-worker, volunteering for a project or speaking up about a new idea. There's nothing good about being a power-hungry Paul.

The death of the feudal leader in you births the cutting-edge leader who is:

- **Passionate and Committed.** They work with a sense of purpose. Those around them recognize and respect these qualities and become motivated themselves to achieve higher levels. They are facilitators not dictators.
- **Coachable.** They admit they don't know everything,

---

[3]Charles O'Reilly and Jennifer Chatman, 'Transformational Leader or Narcissist? How Grandiose Narcissists Can Create and Destroy Organizations and Institutions', *California Management Review*, Vol. 62(3), Pp. 5–27, 29 April 2020. https://doi.org/10.1177/0008125620914989

recognize their own limitations and encourage constructive feedback from others. They seek role models and mentors, are open to new ideas and are willing to try different ways of doing things.

- **Daring.** They don't automatically accept the traditional ways of doing things. But this is not because they are being difficult. It is because they refuse to blindly accept the norms and are assertive enough to speak up.

- **Kind.** They are effective communicators and can carry good conversations with everyone—from the door attendant to the CEO. They are respectful of others and don't let their ego get in their way. Others enjoy being around them.

- **Independent.** They readily seek advice from others on important decisions but are quite comfortable making up their own mind and drawing their own conclusions.

- **Confident.** They quickly identify the things that need to be done and undertake those tasks with minimal prompting and supervision. They don't wait to be told what to do.

- **Technically-Able.** A technically skilled leader sees the bigger picture that technology can play in an organization. It is one of the critical skills that a leader should possess.

- **Think Digital.** Cutting-edge visionaries will be quick to scan the overall landscape and be fully aware of the latest developments in their industry and even in others. Such leaders are conscious of the role they have in terms of driving transformation within the business. They have sensitive antennae, that allows them to stay ahead of the curve.

Five Takeaways for You To Skim Through:

- You have to kill the feudal boss within you to make way for the cutting-edge leader you were always meant to be.

- The cutting-edge leader handles the volatile, complicated, uncertain and ambiguous world with agility, understanding, communication and vision.
- The new-age leader isn't power-hungry, result-driven or an autocrat who only directs his team; he's a democratic servant-leader who lets his teammates make decisions.
- The new-age leader thinks digital and uses technology to the best of his ability.
- The new-age leader is passionate, daring and they are willing to learn and unlearn.

2

BELIEVE IT, YOU REALLY ARE A LEADER

*If your actions inspire others to dream more, learn more,
do more and become more, you are a leader.*

—Dolly Parton

Before you get into wanting to be a new-age leader, you have to know whether you even view yourself as leadership material. Do you think you're a little too soft or shy to manage a team? Do you think your introversion will never let you be like those charismatic business leaders you see on magazines and televisions? Is your idea of 'a natural born leader' holding you back?

There are students in every class who volunteer to organize field trips or lead the pep rally. For team leaders, class officers and club presidents, they're an obvious choice. That wasn't me, by the way. Not at all.

When it came time for someone to take charge, I was more likely to sit back to see who else came forward. If no one else would do it, then I'd stand up. It wasn't that I didn't care about the project; I just didn't see myself as 'leadership' material. I associated leaders with people who were confident, outgoing and persuasive—all the things I wasn't. This perception unfortunately carried over into my work life, too. I took leadership positions only if no one else wanted to step up. However, I won't let you make the same errors.

Too often I hear the word 'leader' misused. Many business professionals, sadly, do not consider themselves as leaders, owing to the fact that the term 'leader' is often associated with persons in positions of official authority. This is a myth that stifles achievement in all areas of life. Know that anyone who claims to have been 'born a leader' is lying. No one is born a leader; instead, they grow into it. While some of history's greatest leaders were born with leadership DNA and attributes, they still had to work hard to improve their abilities throughout time. Also, gone are the days when your employees are cool with their leader being really good at work but terrible at everything else. That inspires very few. Great leaders take care of their people and themselves. So, if you're a good person who cares about others' benefit, you're already winning the battle against so-called 'natural and charismatic' leaders who only care about themselves.

This question of whether leaders are born or made has been debated for decades. *The Leadership Quarterly* conducted some excellent research and discovered that 24 per cent of our leadership comes from our genes, while the remaining 76 per cent is learned or developed.[4] I've learned over the last few years that successful leaders don't have to fit a specific model. Introverted leaders, for example, can be as productive as their extroverted counterparts—if not more so. While all excellent leaders need to be knowledgeable in certain areas, they aren't always the

---

[4]Jan-Emmanuel De Neve et al, 'Born to lead? A twin design and genetic association study of leadership role occupancy', *The Leadership Quarterly*, Vol. 24, Pp. 45-60, 2013. https://doi.org/10.1016/j.leaqua.2012.08.001

sharpest person in the room. (More often than not, they simply know how to surround themselves with smarter people.) When you boil it down to its simplest elements, leadership comes down to knowing yourself, knowing your team, knowing your competition and knowing your gameplan.

It doesn't take a rocket scientist to figure out that each of us has the capacity to be a leader. The difference between Dolly Parton and you, on the other hand, is the bravery to take a risk and the will to succeed. Do you ever lay awake at night thinking about the promotion you should go for but can't, because you don't think you would be fit for it? Think again, here are some indications that you are a great leader and you don't even know it yet.

We all make the mistake of believing that in order to be a leader, you must be born with the ability to lead, be inclined to leadership or have a leadership role. We consider leadership to be a term that must be acquired or deserved. Leaders, on the other hand, are rarely, if ever, born leaders. If we had to pinpoint a single factor that produces leaders, it would most likely be a combination of situation and perseverance. There are a lot of leaders among us—in all kinds of people, places and positions. Some of the most powerful leaders you'll ever encounter are completely unaware of their own power.

Thinking of yourself as a leader is, first and foremost, a key to becoming one. It's critical to establish this before you start running down the ego road. Others determine whether or not you are a leader. Most people, on the other hand, struggle because they believe that leadership is just for certain kinds and types of people, not for them. Also, keep in mind that everyone is supposed to lead in some fashion—whether it's in their personal lives, at business or at home.

So, whether leading comes naturally or not, it should be

evident now that you're called to lead in some part of your journey, so you might as well become a better leader. You've just stepped into this exciting new role as leader, and mixed with the feeling of accomplishment, pride and enthusiasm may be a little apprehension. After all, you've never led a team before, and you may not feel like a true leader just yet—especially if you are managing people who are older or more experienced than you. I'm here to tell you to take it easy on yourself. First, you received a promotion, so someone within your organization has faith in you to do the job. Somewhere along the way, you proved that you have what it takes to lead a team. Beyond that, you can be a leader—if you just behave like one. It really is that simple, and while it may take time to build your status as a great leader, you can start working toward that today. Firstly, realize you have all the potential to be a good leader (even if you do not address audiences like Steve Jobs or think you aren't as witty and cool as Elon Musk) How, you may ask? You *are* a leader (and you don't even realize it) if you possess these traits:

1) **You have an open mind and seek out other people's opinions.** If people are drawn to you because you are open to other people's opinions, you are a leader. If you have found yourself listening to someone, tell you on how to do things more efficiently and take it as constructive criticism, I applaud you.

    The best leaders aren't lone wolves. They take their team members' suggestions and concerns into consideration before acting. If you stand up for your own ideas but fairly weigh every option before proceeding, then odds are, your co-workers consider you as leadership material.

2) **You *actually* know your colleagues.** It's difficult to effectively dictate when you know nothing about the people who work

for you. Every good leader takes the time to get to know the people on their team, because, as Motus Global CEO Joe Nolan said, 'You can know your mission and vision, but it is equally, if not more, important to know your people.' The more you know about your employees, the more you can utilize their skills and strong suits in the workplace (and avoid their weaknesses). You also build relationships organically, even if you're shy or reserved—you know people in other departments and you've gotten to know customers and colleagues. You know how to foster genuine connections and how to encourage successful teamwork.

3) **You are welcoming and accessible.** If you find yourself giving advice to your friends and co-workers more than you are taking it, it means that they value your opinion and are the go-to person for help. Being approachable is an important quality for a leader to have because no one really wants to work for someone without an open-door policy. People trust your judgment and confide in you: take pride in that. You're a great listener—you listen to understand rather than to reply. When peers come to you with problems, you help them figure out an answer that works for them.

4) **You are a pillar of support.** If people rely on you, it follows that they trust you to follow through and deliver on your promises. If you hold yourself accountable and demonstrate the kind of day-in, day-out responsibility that leads others to trust you, you are a leader.

5) **Your views and ideas matter.** This is probably the most obvious sign that your peers view you as a leader. Whether or not you're the boss, you're a fixture in the office when it comes to giving insight and ideas. If this sounds like you, then your co-workers clearly value your wisdom.

6) **Your boss stops guiding you at every step.** 'But wait, isn't that

a bad thing?' is what you're probably asking yourself. I say, 'Not exactly.' 'Sometimes, bosses want to see how proactive and self-initiating their future leaders are. Those who need less care and feeding may have the edge over those who need constant reinforcement and direction to be productive,' Jim Morris writes for the Daily Muse.[5] Having your supervisor 'neglect' you sometimes might not be the best feeling in the world, but it's probably a pretty good sign. They know you can handle things on your own. Cheer up.

7) **You don't panic in times of crisis.** Maintaining professional composure is an important skill that many leaders possess and that many employers seek. It's critical to remain calm and in command of the situation. You have more patience than most if you have found yourself calmly nodding while listening to someone who is clearly furious and screaming at you.

8) **You take on duties when nobody else does.** There are some days where it just sucks to live, and you want to just lay in bed. You want to stay put, eat your meals there and sleep again. You shove whatever is bothering you aside and force yourself out of bed because you have obligations. You have people depending on you, and you have tasks to complete that will not be completed by themselves. Some people never get out of bed and put off completing duties until another day, but not you. This is what it means to be accountable. When no one else wants to be responsible, leaders must step forward.

9) **You're not power-hungry.** In an article for Inc., Les

---

[5]Jim Morris, '8 Surefire Signs You're on the Path to Becoming a Real Leader', The Muse, https://www.themuse.com/advice/8-surefire-signs-youre-on-the-path-to-becoming-a-real-leader, Accessed on 1 March 2022.

McKeown wrote that there's a difference between take-charge-type posers and real leaders: 'Always opinionated, usually impatient and frequently brusque, these gotta-be-in-fronters get so used to other people describing them as natural born leaders that sooner or later—to their own and everyone else's detriment—they begin to believe it.'[6] Real leaders only take the helm when it's necessary. People generally prefer selfless leaders. Over ambitious and grasping ones (remember power-hungry Paul?)—yeah, everyone hates him.

10) **You're not afraid of working hard.** When people think of Fortune 500 CEOs, they think of a man in a suit who comes into the workplace once a week merely to put on a show. Effective CEOs, on the other hand, are not like this. Good leaders, on the other hand, are like new employees in that they are the first to arrive and the last to leave. They know that the hard work never stops and that everyone needs to contribute in order for things to get done.

11) **You are not afraid of messing up.** A little bit of humility goes a long way—but if you're a born leader, then you probably already know this. Naturally, employees appreciate superiors who take their feedback into consideration and, above all else, can admit when they're wrong.

12) **You don't constantly crave validation.** I'm not saying you defer it. I'm saying you vehemently stop craving it altogether. Over time, credit becomes less and less valuable to leaders. In its place comes a desire to execute the job you were hired to do to the best of your abilities. Great leaders, for

---

[6]Les McKeown, '3 Signs You're Meant to Be a Leader', *Inc.*, https://www.inc.com/les-mckeown/3-signs-youre-a-true-leader.html, Accessed on 1 March 2022.

the most part, detach their activities from their outcomes and take satisfaction from the task itself.

13) **You care about how you make others feel.** You understand the people that are like you—primarily as a result of how you make them feel and not how you look or how smart or cool you appear to be. It's fine to have an edge and it's good to be bold, but good leaders are keenly aware of how people feel in their presence.

14) **You *love* learning.** Do you have a habit of rereading books in order to grasp all of the information on the pages? This could be an indication that you were born to lead—as natural leaders are continually seeking new information in order to grow. Leaders understand the necessity of expanding their minds, whether they're learning about their area or just consuming knowledge for the sake of absorbing knowledge.

15) **You're authentic and know your job well.** A good leader doesn't have to give amazing speeches, look flawless or even have a ton of charisma. People will perceive you as a promising leader if you have insightful solutions and prepare well for workplace projects. Instead of trying to wow others with fake charisma, focus on being the best you can be at your job. Voila, you are leadership material.

Ask yourself these questions to know where you stand in the cutting-edge leadership race:

- Would I want to work with myself?
- What are my strengths and weaknesses? (Cliched but important.)
- Am I using my time to the best of my ability?
- What did I do to help my team today?

- Do I lift as I climb?
- Do I know what I don't know and let others know?
- Do I invite others in?
- Is my voice loud when others are quiet?
- Am I providing reality and hope?
- Do I truly love my work and understand my peers?
- Can I make tough decisions?
- Am I ready to take accountability?
- Do I have a high tolerance for uncertainty?

Five Takeaways for You To Skim Through:

- The first step to being a leader is realizing you *are* one, irrespective of what your position in the office is.
- Your leadership potential doesn't have to do with how loud or assertive you are, rather, how well you work with others, solve issues and handle yourself during crisis.
- Leaders do not have to give long speeches in front of thousands or have to be cool like Elon Musk. A new-age leader just needs to master his/her people, work and technology.
- Softness isn't a con but a pro for new-age leadership. Nobody in this era wants leaders who yell and bang their fists against desks. Use your softness to your advantage and charm your teammates.
- Similarly, even introverts can lead as well as extroverts. They're brilliant thinkers, active listeners and walk their talk.

3

LEAD OFF-THE-WALL

Power isn't control at all - power is strength, and giving
that strength to others. A leader isn't someone who forces
others to make him stronger; a leader is someone willing to
give his strength to others that they may have the strength
to stand on their own.[7]

—Beth Revis, American author

'But I still don't feel like a leader!' you may be thinking. Probably because you're not smooth with words or 'in-your-face' magnetic? Or maybe you cannot give moving public speeches that birth an uproar of applause?

Firstly, find out whether you're an 'innie' or an 'outie'. I'm not referring to your bellybuttons; I'm referring to your leadership style. Do you consider yourself to be an introvert or an extrovert? Leadership, like personalities, comes in a variety of forms. Introversion or extroversion has nothing to do with how shy or social you are; it has everything to do with how you get your energy.

An introvert's primary source of energy, stimulation, comes

---

[7]Beth Revis, Across the Universe: 1, *Razorbill*, 2011.

from within, from their inner world of thoughts, ideas and reflections. They focus their attention and energy within, receiving energy from their ideas, memories and feelings. The exterior world, the world of people and things, provides crucial stimulation for extroverts. They focus their energy and attention outward, gaining energy from connecting with others and taking action. Both have their own strengths and weaknesses. You cannot possibly compare Spiderman with Batman, right?

Yes, even introverts and shy people can be *equally* good leaders. 'I think most people have unrealistic ideas about leadership,' Hugh Kearns said in an interview with *Science* magazine. 'They tend to think they have to be Nelson Mandela or some such inspirational character. In reality, leadership is much more mundane: for example, preparing for your meeting, communicating with people, and listening.'[8] I cannot help but agree. You aren't a leader in a sci-fi or historical film, you're a realistic business leader, and so, you can be a cutting-edge leader even if you're shy or a person of few words. Remember that.

How Do You Lead as an Introvert?

There are two common misconceptions that come up over and over again in leadership conversations. One is that the best leaders are naturally extroverted. The other is that introverts are weaker leaders because they 'don't like people'.

While introverts prefer their alone time, they aren't inherently opposed to social events; rather, they require space to recuperate after being around others. When you're an introvert

---

[8]Sharon Ann Holgate, 'Enhance Your Career With Leadership Skills', *Science*, 23 March 2012, https://www.science.org/content/article/enhance-your-career-leadership-skills, Accessed on 1 March 2022.

in a leadership role—where you spend a lot of time attending meetings and planning with your team—this can be a difficult balance to strike.

In the business world, extroverts are more expected to serve in leadership positions, because they're more outspoken public speakers and more commanding in meetings. However, some of the biggest companies on the planet were founded and led by introverts, including Jeff Bezos, Warren Buffett, Tim Cook and Bill Gates. You didn't know that? Believe it, these iconic leaders are introverted, just like you.

Studies have shown that about 50 per cent of the US population are introverts, and the increasingly positive view of introversion has allowed introverts to feel more confident about being leaders in the workplace. Despite popular belief, introverts can make terrific leaders. In the job, a tendency to be more reserved and silent can be beneficial. Introverted leaders are excellent listeners who pay attention to their staff, clients and consumers. They also consider the team's goals and difficulties in order to develop intelligent answers and ideas. Introverts in positions of leadership are more likely to let others shine and recognize their accomplishments.

How Do You Take On Leadership as an Introvert ?

1) **Your belief is your anchor.** Amy P. Kelly, Human Resources and Organizational Development Executive, as well as a Certified High-Performance Executive Coach, said that, 'When a leader has belief, it's a magnet for others to want to be part of it. Conversely, if you don't have belief, no one else around you can.'[9] Not only is she correct, but it

---

[9]Amy Kelly, 'Great Leaders Start with Belief with Amy Kelly' [podcast],

highlights the essential nature of self-belief and the belief in others as a critical element of leadership. Because as the saying goes, 'If you don't believe in yourself, then who will believe in you?'

Even though you probably don't feel like an invincible leader, know you have one inside of you, irrespective of your shyness. Yes, you *are* a leader. Own it.

2) **Your silence and observation are golden,** *truly.* One of the greatest assets of an introverted leader is their ability to listen carefully before speaking. That means you may gather feedback from your team and use it to help you grow as a leader, rather than reacting or following your gut sense. You may thoroughly analyse every position while you're attentively listening. While introverts prefer not to speak up as much as extroverts, they are better at hearing and absorbing information on the other side of the conversation. In leadership, people can use listening to gather additional ideas from others and put the finest ones into action.

'Listening comes more easily when you spend less time talking,' entrepreneur and author Jeff Booth wrote in Fast Company. 'It isn't just about hearing someone's words— either a good listener pays attention to the deeper message that's not being said and develops empathy for the person speaking. This can pay real dividends inside businesses, even if they're harder to see from the outside.'[10]

Season 28, Episode 9 (10 February 2021), The John Eades Podcast, https://followmylead.libsyn.com/great-leaders-start-with-belief-with-amy-kelly, Accessed on 1 March 2022.

[10]Jeff Booth, 'How I've Learned To Lead As An Introverted CEO', *Fast Company*, 6 March 2016, https://www.fastcompany.com/3060536/how-ive-learned-to-lead-as-an-introverted-ceo, Accessed on 1 March 2022.

3) **Show them you are concerned.** Nobody wants extroverts or charismatic leaders who just won't stop harping on about how they 'built their own empires with their own hands' or 'rise and grind everyday'.

   You may talk less or be shy, but you are so much more powerful when you show others you care. There aren't many leadership hacks but simply demonstrating you care about others in each interaction might be one. Whether leadership comes naturally or not, if people don't think you care about them as human beings, you won't go far as a leader.

   Alongside humility, empathy is arguably one of the most prominent traits in introverted people, and this is especially useful for introverts in leading roles as it can help develop trust, loyalty and improve communication.

4) **You know it: actions speak louder than words.** Introverts are not as proficient at being heard during 'heat of the moment' meetings where the louder, more extroverted people are usually dominating. Introverts can counteract that by ensuring they 'knock it out of the park' in regards to their performance on both the business and leadership fronts. Be known as someone who is competent, credible and consistently delivers.

5) **'I think, therefore I am.'** Introverts are also known for being reflective, which can be a positive trait for a leader. That's an introverted feeling you can trust when it comes to making key business judgments. Before making any adjustments, spend some time alone to think over your decisions and evaluate fresh ideas for a defined period of time. Instead of plunging into new activities before you're comfortable with them, this may be a better option for introverts.

   When you're exploring new ideas or making significant judgments, it's also a good idea to write them down. When there are visuals involved, introverts often think more clearly. Writing things down can also help you organize your thoughts and prevent you from becoming overwhelmed by too many ideas.

6) **Don't let labels get to you.** The biggest thing that holds back introverted leaders is an incorrect impression of what leadership and introversion are by both themselves and others. Ignore the label and studies that suggest introverts make excellent leaders. Simply take a confident step into your own. Others would not look to you to lead if they did not trust you. Just go for it.

7) **Communicate effectively.** I cannot stress upon this enough— communication isn't so much about speaking and replying, as it is about being receptive. As opposed to extroverts who tend to think out loud, introverts really take their time to internally craft a very specific and crystal-clear message that will get the job done from the get-go. 'That's why I think that introverts have tremendous leadership potential,' Solomon Thimothy, president of OneIMS, explains. 'In addition to being effective communicators, they can organize the work of the entire team hyper-efficiently and smoothly, which is a great advantage for any business,' he says.

8) **Lift the other quiet ones up.** The quiet, reflective manner of introverts often means that we can fade into the background as more vocal team members articulate their views. Introverts need time to process their thoughts before speaking, and often this 'processing time' means that we miss out on sharing our opinions because the moment has passed.

As an introverted leader, it's easier for you to identify other introverts on your team. What someone else may dismiss as lack of participation or not want to share opinions could actually just be an introvert taking the time to think before speaking.

To be an effective leader, make the effort to draw out other introverts on your team and give them space to contribute in their own way. Perhaps they are uncomfortable sharing their thoughts with the entire group, so instead you could arrange for a one-on-one meeting to get their feedback. Alternatively, allow team members to e-mail you their views after the meeting instead of immediately closing the discussion.

9) **Prepare for meetings beforehand.** Even for introverted leaders, occasional meetings with staff can still be beneficial. However, if you go into those meetings unprepared, you're more likely to become overwhelmed or have poor communication with team members. Instead, even for informal meetings, jot down some thoughts or create an agenda or presentation so that you can stay on track.

Also, don't overbook yourself with meetings; else, you'll burn out quickly. Introverts need alone or quiet time to refuel. Extroverts get their energy from being around other people. Introverted leaders should avoid organizing too many activities in a single day or week. Meetings and conferences should be spaced out so that you may enjoy them and not feel drained by the end of the week. Having scheduled times for 'open door policies' will also allow for reflection and recharging.

10) **Keep it small, large isn't always good.** It can also be beneficial for introverted leaders to communicate with team members in a one-on-one setting. This can help you get ideas and feedback from everyone on your team, not just the ones who are most likely to speak up during meetings. 'Introverts gain energy, wisdom and momentum from within, while

extroverts are energized by people around them. Both are strategic, visionary and effective. I'd recommend one-on-one lunches, individual meetings and small group reflections for introverted leaders so they shine—and so people hear their true thinking. Large group meetings are inevitable but may not be most impactful for introverts,' suggests Joanne Markow, GreenMason.[11]

Seek out small groups that can help you achieve your vision. Find strategic alliances within your company who can help you bring about the change you want to see. Form small groups of two or three people to work on specific problems. This will allow you to participate in the topic and immerse yourself in it. Finally, it's a fantastic method to gain buy-in and establish rapport.

Tips for Extroverts To Lead (Because Extroverts Aren't Naturally Perfect Leaders, Trust Me)

Michael Wilmot, an academic, argues that extroversion is linked with a greater motivation to achieve positive goals; for example, a desired reward through work.[12] It's also linked to having more good emotions on a regular basis. Employees who are happy are more likely to work harder and are regarded to be better

---

[11]Forbes Coaches Council, 'Nine Tips To Help Introverted Leaders Succeed In The Workplace', Forbes, 2 March 2018, https://www.forbes.com/sites/forbescoachescouncil/2018/03/02/nine-tips-to-help-introverted-leaders-succeed-in-the-workplace/?sh=1edfb1104300, Accessed on 1 March 2022.

[12]Don Campbell, 'Extroverts enjoy four key advantages according to a new UTSC study. Here they are.', University of Toronto Scarborough News, 29 May 2019, https://utsc.utoronto.ca/news-events/breaking-research/extroverts-enjoy-four-key-advantages-according-new-utsc-study-here-they-are, Accessed on 1 March 2022.

leaders as a result. Extroverts' positive demeanour also helps to buffer them from stress or adverse experiences at work.

Since extroverts enjoy the company of others, they tend to adapt better to different social situations and are better persuaders, which is a strong leadership skill.

However, not all is rosy or a cake-walk for an extrovert as a leader, too. Here are some tips for you to not sabotage your leadership potential through too much extroversion.

- Ask yourself, '*Why am I talking right now?* Is this really required or productive?'
- *Learn when to stop talking* and don't interrupt when someone else speaks.
- *Try to listen more* and reflect on what you just heard.
- Provide opportunity for other people to contribute.
- *Ask more questions and really listen.* Resist the urge to immediately start providing your opinion. Notice in meetings with your team and how much time you might be talking relative to others. Just because you are the leader or manager, don't assume that it should be more than others.
- *Tell introverts ahead of time what you'd like to discuss.* Don't side-line them just because they're shy or quieter.
- *Be careful what you say.* What you say has a lot of weight behind it. If you talk out loud too much, you may appear to seem as indecisive. If you're going to 'extrovert' or brainstorm ideas, make sure others are aware of your plans.
- *Be careful of oversharing.* Not everything needs to be discussed out loud.
- *Don't claim to be the smartest in the room.* Extroverts are usually confident, but being overconfident is just plain bad leadership.

- *Use your extroversion to loosen up introverts* on your team. Trust me, introverts feel wonderful when they're heard and recognized.
- *Pause.* Extroverts have a habit of filling silences with words that aren't always meaningful, relevant or even required. Silence seems to make them uncomfortable. That isn't good for you. Learn to take a breath and consider before speaking.
- *Don't be loud all the time.* Extroverts have a tendency to talk more and louder than others. To put it another way, they tend to occupy more 'verbal space' than others. While that can be good at times, eating into others' space is going to lead you nowhere despite your smooth-talking and charm.
- *Mean what you say.* When you speak, say what is important and mean what you say. You don't need to use many words and you don't need to deliver them loudly or in a caustic fashion. You do need to express ideas and directives clearly, set expectations in understandable terms, but you do not need to shout or sugar-coat to accomplish this.
- *Don't be obsessed with external validation.* Extroverts love being praised for their work and achievements; however, constantly wanting to be recognized will make you seem desperate for compliments. Work because you are passionate about what you do, not because you want to impress others.

Are You 'Too Soft' To Be a Leader?

James Kavanaugh once suggested that there are 'those too gentle to live among the wolves.'[13] This doesn't really apply to today's

---

[13]James Kavanaugh, *There Are Men Too Gentle to Live Among Wolves,* Steven J. Nash Publishing, 1991.

cutting-edge organization. I believe that the 'wolves' have had their day, and we need to make way for a new breed of leaders— the soft leader. Today, we need a special brand of leader who can create a real sense of community and commitment in our organizations.

Softly spoken leaders have it tough. When many people think of leadership, they often still think of the ambitious, strong, forceful person smashing down barriers and screaming orders. If someone is soft spoken or doesn't stomp on other people's throats to get to the top, sometimes people don't consider them to be 'leadership material'. Softly spoken leaders are talked over in meetings, ignored and can find it hard to get their point across. By comparison, their loud, forceful counterparts may be perceived as more capable and driven. However, often the loudest people in the room are full of hot air or just speaking for the sake of it. And if you look closely, the quiet achievers might just be your best leaders. As Dr Henry Cloud has said, 'I try to go hard on the issue and soft on the person.'[14] *That*, in my opinion, is absolutely magnetic.

Command-and-control leadership is no longer effective. Currently, trust-and-track leadership is productive. Soft leadership is the way of the future. Because the world is changing so quickly, so are the knowledge, skills and talents required of employees. To stay up with the rapid developments in technology, employees are reinventing themselves. They are also more focused on their work and are willing to sacrifice their families in order to advance in their careers. Their hopes and expectations are increasing. As a result, senior executives must reinvent their leadership styles, tools and strategies in order to manage their

---

[14]Henry Cloud, *Boundaries for Leaders: Results, Relationships, and Being Ridiculously in Charge,* Harper Business, 2013.

teams in the digital age.

Being a leader, it is not disadvantageous to be soft-spoken and courteous. Leaders that yell, cajole, belittle and demean their subordinates exist. These leaders are well-known and consistently provide outcomes. It's a different matter whether or not those outcomes are desirable. Leaders that are soft-spoken and courteous have an edge when practising genuine leadership.

'Power is of two kinds,' Mahatma Gandhi correctly distinguished. 'One is obtained by the fear of punishment and the other by acts of love. Power based on love is 1,000 times more effective and permanent than the one derived from fear of punishment.' Hard leaders are frequently self-focused, whereas soft leaders are centred on others—and the former has no place in the next-gen workplace. As we form more remote teams and engage a multigenerational workforce, the need to connect people to a cause bigger than themselves becomes more important.

Soft leaders have a critical role in fostering a sense of importance and belonging. They're also a rare breed. When was the last time you observed a leader put his or her staff first on their priority list? When was the last time you heard a leader talk about compassion and caring as though it meant something? When was the last time you saw a CEO make a significant personal sacrifice for the sake of the company's lowest-paid employee? Time for *you* to fill this void and be the cutting-edge, soft leader.

Here are some tips to becoming a soft-leader:

- **Take Pride in Being Gentle and Compassionate:** The world has enough dominant, loud and aggressive leaders. Let's try something different. Telling yourself that you are softly spoken may be a limiting belief. This can be limiting because you are subconsciously thinking that you should fit the 'normal' leadership stereotypes: strong, bold, opinionated, forceful, confident. You might not feel like any of those leadership words apply to you.

So, let's reframe the situation. If you're softly spoken, you probably speak quietly and don't speak all the time. This just means you are more selective about your words when you do speak. Being selective is a good thing. You don't just pollute the air with words. You add *real value* to the conversation.

- **The Triangle:** I often talk about the three points of the triangle that leaders must serve: your employees, your customers and your superiors. A considerate leader looks to achieve wins for all three as often as possible. When both the employees and customers win, the leader most often does as well. When you demonstrate to your people that you take their needs into consideration when making decisions, even when you cannot give them what they want, they will respect your decisions more.

- **Let Your Work Be Loud for You:** Sounds obvious? I know, but it's true. Doing great work gives you credibility. Credibility starts to give you respect. Then, people are more likely to listen. Even if people say you are 'too quiet', or 'not ambitious enough', it ultimately doesn't matter. Nobody fires someone who does great work. Doing great work provides you with more time to build your confidence. Once you're regarded as a high performer, people tend to feel more compelled to listen. You will stand up and shout 'Hey, I've got something to say!' Not literally, of course—but you get the idea.

- **Your Listening Skills Make You Glow:** Listening is an essential skill for a new-age leader. The most important lesson acquired is to pay attention to what the other person is saying and then say something like, 'What I hear you say is (state what you heard).' This demonstrates to others that we are paying attention, and it keeps the emphasis on the genuine, relevant concerns. From here, adding our thoughts, ideas and suggested actions, a productive give-and-take occurs. You may even find that others will adopt your approach.

- **Solve, Solve, Solve:** The best way to keep focused is to keep repeating quietly in our mind: solve the issue, solve the issue, solve the issue. It may sound corny, but it works. It keeps our thoughts, words and actions focused on the right things. It delivers the discipline of interaction—the discipline of going hard on the issue and soft on the person.
- **Push Yourself To Be Firm When Needed:** This may be the hardest part because while you can be soft spoken and considerate, you cannot be timid or lacking in conviction. Your people are counting on you and if you let yourself be rolled over by events or other forces, your people will be left to face the full force of the hardships that come their way. Stand firm when you need to do so, and advocate for what's best for your people, your customers and the company. There are times to compromise and times to be wrong and change course, but do not fold at the first sign of resistance or opposition. Also, don't make compromises or sacrifices just to keep your teammates happy. Pushovers are never leaders.
- **Don't Be a People-Pleaser:** Leaders are placed under a tremendous amount of pressure to be relatable, likeable and nice. Many yield to this instinct, because it feels much easier to be liked. Doing everything in your power to be a nice and friendly leader for your team? Well, here's the ugly truth: your team isn't going to like you all the time.

Few people want to be the bad guy, especially the soft-hearted ones. Leaders, on the other hand, are expected to make difficult decisions in the best interests of the company or team. Being overly pleasant can lead to laziness, inefficiency, irresponsibility and harm to persons and organizations. Talk about difficult things. 'Why is it getting delayed?', 'Why are we failing to complete this deadline?', 'Where do you think you went wrong?', etc. are some tough questions you could pose, in a tone that is soft. You will have to talk about the tough stuff sometime, because if you don't, things will go the opposite of what you planned.

- **Don't Lie or Sugar-coat:** Sugar-coated words appeal to all of us. However, it does not operate well in the job. As a leader, you must communicate with your employees what they require. It's pointless to sugar-coat bad criticism. Instead, assist them in finding opportunities for growth. Point out major areas of improvement in your team members' performance and tell them what needs to be altered if you want them to be more productive.

Remember:

- By not giving that employee feedback, you are restricting their development.
- If you don't correct your new co-worker on how they're pronouncing your name, you'll undoubtedly cause them humiliation later.
- Keeping a slacker employee on the job? You're sending a negative message to high performers and possibly keeping someone in a role that they don't truly love.
- How about letting a meeting go off track resulting in it running over—you will either have wasted a lot of time or

maybe not reached the outcomes required.

• Perhaps you've agreed to something with a client that you know might not get the best results, but it's too late to change now because of the fear of losing face. Think about the time, focus and potential costs that will be lost.

Be the Girl-Boss You've Always Dreamt of Being

This one's for the talented ladies out there: you are no less than *anyone else* in the workplace. I'm here to tell you why and how you be a true cutting-edge leader and the superwoman the world needs. Sheryl Sandberg has stated that 'We need women at all levels, including the top, to change the dynamic, reshape the conversation, to make sure women's voices are heard and heeded, not overlooked and ignored,'[15] and I personally believe she only spoke facts.

During uncertain times, we often see calls for strong leadership. During crisis, it's only natural to move towards strength—whether consciously or unconsciously. Yet, research has found that *both genders* typically equate strong leadership with confidence, forcefulness and decisiveness—yes, these traits aren't just limited to men.

Think about it: the Covid-19 pandemic has shone a spotlight onto the issue of leadership and many have reconsidered what constitutes 'strong' leadership. Many of the countries which have taken decisive action and been praised for their handling of the

[15]Sheryl Sandberg, 'Barnard College Commencement 2011',HuffPost, 13 June 2011, https://www.huffpost.com/entry/barnard-college-commencem_b_876352, Accessed on 1 March 2022.

crisis—from New Zealand, Germany, Finland to Taiwan—are helmed by *women*. Women leaders who have broken the glass ceiling in medium-sized, non-traditional organizations have shown us that great leaders don't come from one mould or formula. They have proven that the traditional command-and-control style of handling workers is so passé. Let me tell you why the cutting-edge business world of today's times needs more women leaders:

- Women leaders are master communicators—their soft-skills and interpersonal interaction are absolute weapons in the organization.
- They make great listeners and are nurturing.
- Woman leaders are great at showcasing empathy, which is a must for the new-age leader.
- Women leaders are great interactors and transformational guides.
- Women also happen to be master multi-taskers.
- They can wear many hats, from being a mum, a wife to a professional, all at once.
- Their emotional intelligence makes them magnetic to new-age workers.
- They are creative and collaborative.
- They're super servant leaders.[16]

---

[16]Servant leadership is a concept of leadership in which the leader's primary objective is to serve others. This is in contrast to traditional leadership, in which the leader's primary concern is the success of his or her firm or organization.

Here Are Some Hacks for You To Shower Your Girl-Power in the Workplace

- Don't be afraid to take up space. You have a unique range of gifts to offer the world, so share those gifts.
- Don't feel anxious about your abilities. You were chosen for this job and this position for a damn good reason. Show your confidence.
- Stop being 'sorry' for the smallest of things; you're a leader and you're going to have to take tough decisions that might bruise fragile egos—if you know what I mean.
- You don't have to be bossy, rude or condescending to show strength. In fact, the strongest leaders I know are inclusive, collaborative, kind and thoughtful. Your feminine coaching, communication and empathy are like Thanos' gauntlet.
- Surround yourself with people who believe in you, support you and remind you of your strengths.
- Charm your peers through your empathy. Historically, women have struggled at times to be heard in the workplace. Perhaps, they can't find a way to join a lively conversation or have experienced their idea being stolen in a team meeting. Leaders who have been through this are often better at recognizing when it happens to others—and doing something about it.
- Do your fellow females a favour and offer support, not criticism. When you see another woman co-worker succeeding, cheer her on. She's paving the way for you and future women to come. So offer her your hand, your applause and your generosity. That way, you create an army of girl-bosses.
- It's easier to lead when doing what you love. Reflect on what brings you joy and then go for it—create an opportunity

to inspire others.

- Create networks of contacts who will be your profit-pillars. Women are naturally great at socializing—might as well use that at work, too? Always gain and train allies to support your agenda.
- Overcommunicate. Remind your team why their work matters. Find something that makes each and every one of your team member's work meaningful. Your goal should be to make them feel as though they are doing something greater than working for a pay check.
- Don't forget leading yourself and your growth in the process of keeping your peers happy. Find a balance.
- Stop making yourself small so that someone else feels big. It is not your job. At the same time, remember to charm others through your humility. People love that.
- Make your cake and eat it, too. Yes, you can have both a family, a personal life and a professional life. You're more powerful than you realize. Invest beyond your work into your mental health, your physical fitness and your loved ones. Makes you truer, more human and hence, makes you an attractive modern leader.

Five Takeaways for You To Skim Through:

- Don't run away from leading teams because you're an introvert. Studies tell us introverts lead teams equally well (if not better) through their listening skills, observations and genuine concern for peers.
- Extroverts have an upper-edge as they're good with socializing and communicating. However, too much of talking and energy can lead you to overcommit and drain yourself.

- Women leaders are absolute powerhouses because of their emotional intelligence, nurturing, gentleness and coaching skills. They make wonderful, new-age transformational leaders.
- Don't think leadership is just about being loud, aggressive or authoritative. The new leadership requires new values such as empathy, listening, understanding and softness.
- Now you know why you are a leader, even if you don't feel like one due to your soft voice or your shyness, perhaps.

4

LEADING A MIX

*A diverse mix of voices leads to better discussions,
decisions, and outcomes for everyone.*

—Sundar Pichai, Indian-American Business Executive
and ex-CEO, Google, present-day CEO, Alphabet Inc.

As a leader, you want all of your employees to be at their best in
terms of energy, efficiency and motivation, which can be difficult
when you're heading a group of introverts and extroverts. How
do you deal with such a diverse range of personalities and work
styles? How can you entice introverts to speak out and extroverts
to listen? What is the most effective approach to change your
leadership style so that it benefits everyone?

For the Introspective Introverts

- **Firstly, recognize them.** Your new employee, Maria is an
  introvert. She won't be the first one to speak up. Instead,
  she'll listen more than talk. But when she does speak, she'll
  ask questions intended for clarification and avoid long,
  dragged-out comments.

- Maria pays attention to details.
- Maria doesn't reveal much emotion.
- Maria is more methodical and structured in how she likes to complete tasks.
- Maria doesn't need a lot of interaction with people. She wants to be able to ask questions and understand her task and then focus on her task alone.

- **However, don't box Maria within labels.** While it's wonderful to recognize an employee's personality, making them conscious of that will make them withdraw even further. Extroverts and introverts are not chosen personalities. Introverts, like left-handed people, were born that way. Because being an introvert isn't a disease, don't try to 'fix' employees like Maria. Accept them for who they are.
- **Embrace Maria (not literally).** There is nothing to change in Maria. People are simply different, and these differences make the world the way it is. Let them grow as much as possible—both as introverts and as individuals.
- **Coach Maria at *her* pace, not yours.** Introverts may take longer to grasp onto certain things since, a lot of the time, they like to learn and work on their own. Help employees like Maria by encouraging their private nature as well as making it clear that you are always there to help them.
- **Respect Maria's private nature.** An introvert like Maria may not be able to do their best work when surrounded by others and pushing them to do so may end badly. Give introverts the private time and space they need to thrive.
- **Motivate Maria to participate.** Leaders should let everyone on the team know it's okay to be themselves. Each person should understand that they bring a unique style for thinking and sharing. That is, after all, the power of a team.

In meetings or other group settings, some people will talk more and some will talk less. The people who talk more can annoy those who talk less, and the people who talk more may wonder why others aren't talking as much. You should uproot the idea that people who do things differently are wrong or inferior.

Introverts like Maria may try to stay quiet in a meeting. They may not say anything at all if left to their own devices. It's critical, however, that you bring them out and encourage them to speak up. Your team will benefit from their viewpoint and have a deeper understanding of themselves. Speaking up more can also help introverts earn respect from their co-workers and be perceived as more useful to the company. What is the greatest way to get the most out of introverts like Maria?

- Provide discussion topics ahead of time so that they can come to a meeting prepared and not feel rushed.
- Tell them it's fine if they need time to consider an issue or a query.
- After others have given their thoughts, ask them directly what they think.
- Negative input from other team members should be strongly discouraged. It's one thing to objectively explain why an idea may not work, while allowing teasing, sarcasm or personal critiques is another. There should be no obvious impediments to those wanting to contribute.

- **Give them a break.** Allow them to have some much-needed alone time. They require it in the same way that they require food or sleep. Recognize that introverts require some quiet time after a busy activity. It could be a nice night's sleep or simply an uninterrupted break from work. You may be rest assured that they'll be ready to work again after they've recharged.

Some useful communication tips to enchant your introverts:

- Don't disturb them in the middle of a task unless necessary.
- Provide time for them to gather their thoughts and process the information you've delivered.
- Offer thorough answers to their questions and detailed explanations for tasks.
- Choose your words carefully when making corrections. Be tactful.
- Be specific in your praise and in your critiques (without being overly flattering).
- Don't react negatively to a controlled, less emotional response.
- Honour their need for privacy and dignity.
- Don't single them out during group meetings or events. It's their worst nightmare.
- Demonstrate acceptance and tolerance.

How to Channelize Extroverted Energy Towards Success

- **Once again, recognize them.** Your new employee, Chad is an extrovert. He is talkative, sociable, action-oriented, enthusiastic, friendly and out-going. You often find him moving around cubicles, chatting with other co-workers and asking if they need his help. Wherever Chad is, there's a party—jokes, banter, chattering, laughter and energy.

- Chad enjoys being the centre of attention. He loves making others laugh.
- Chad thrives in group work.
- Chad feels isolated by too much time spent alone.
- Chad expresses and organizes ideas and suggestions by talking.
- Chad is all about talking about thoughts and feelings.
- Chad looks to others and outside sources for ideas and inspiration.
- Chad has numerous, broad interests.
- Chad tends to act first before thinking.

- **Take Chad seriously, first and foremost.** When you first meet extroverts, it's likely that they'll be chatty and open, peppering their conversations with jokes, quips and stories. They like to feel comfortable with people, and they think that making little jokes puts you at ease too. But it doesn't mean that they're lightweights in the workplace, that they don't take their work seriously or that they don't have the gravitas that other (less bubbly) people have. So, take employees like Chad seriously—but also leave time for them to bring the fun. They are the ones breaking the ice and the monotony of everyday work.
- **Don't kill Chad's zeal.** Extroverts tend to be energetic and brimming with different ideas. Keep that energy going by encouraging their excitement towards the work they are doing.
- **Let Chad (think) speak to (speak) think.** The very opposite of an introvert, right? Extroverts like Chad recharge their brains when spending time with others, so they usually feel more comfortable coming up with ideas out loud. Let

them be vocal rather than shutting them up (unless their ramblings are nonsensical.)

- **Give Chad air-time.** Set up a frequent face-to-face or video conference with Chad if you notice he's struggling to feel connected. This will allow him to discuss things through with you directly. You can also encourage Chad to use Zoom or Slack breakout groups so that he can chat about his ideas without taking over a team meeting.

Encourage extroverts to return to the office for more 'watercooler moments.' They assist extroverts in establishing spontaneous social connections throughout the day, keeping bosses informed about what's really going on in the organization and fostering trust among teammates.

It's important to also acknowledge that not all extroverts will be returning to the office. Organize more optional hybrid team bonding events, ranging from a Zoom lunch chat to a hybrid meeting happy hour, to prevent excluding those staying at home from social activities. Hybrid lunches have emerged as the new social cafeteria, where team members can meet in person or virtually to share a 15–30-minute meal.

- **Let Chad mix and match**. Monotony is, for Chad, the killer of creativity and productivity. He likes to mix up his day; he moves between listening to music, using meeting rooms when he needs to concentrate, working at his desk to having walking meetings or catch-ups in a nearby coffee shop. He also mixes up his week; and the days where he works from home in glorious, blissful silence are some of his most productive. So, if Chad says he wants to work from home, in a meeting room or café, don't presume it's because he wants to nip off home early or can't be bothered working. It's because, sometimes, the change of scenery is all he needs to get his creative juices flowing.

- **Don't let Chad bite more than he can chew.** Extroverts like Chad will have a lot of energy at work and will feel like they can take on more and more as the day progresses. As a result, some extroverts may have a tendency to say yes to everything and will always want to participate in extracurricular activities, committees, group work and so on. While it's fantastic to encourage all of your employees to take on additional responsibilities, it's also important to make sure that the extroverts you supervise don't overextend themselves.

- **Make use of Chad's chatty charm.** The extroverts should be your go-to employees for public talks, frequent social engagement and after-hours meetings with clients. Comparatively, you may not want to assign Chad to a job that isolates him from the rest of the office. If you need an employee to undertake a week-long research project, consider seeking out an introvert over an extrovert. An extrovert who's not able to discuss the details of their project or collaborate with their peers will take longer to get through the necessary research than an introvert.

Tips To Lead Those Older Than You (Without Making Them Burn in Jealousy)

- **Let them know you *know* they're more experienced.** An older employee has more life experience than a younger employee as he has done more and seen more in his life. Give credit to the older worker for his wisdom and use that experience to your advantage. Encourage other members of your team to recognize the experience and learn from it as well. Respect works like magic when it comes to leading older employees.

- **Don't make them feel ancient**. Do your best not to make people in their 40s feel like they're behind the times with insensitive remarks such as, 'Wow! *You* use Instagram?'

   If you have quality team members in their 50s, consider how lessening their responsibilities—even in their best interest—might be perceived as an attack on their age or capability.

- **Don't get intimidated. Be confident.** Humility is a key part of effective leadership, but you have to know the difference between being humble and undercutting your own knowledge because of your birth year. 'Don't ever apologize for your age,' advises Lindsey Pollak, Career and Workplace Expert, noting that even phrases like, 'I know I've only been here two years,' should not be used too much.[17]

   In some instances, an older employee may challenge your leadership simply because you are younger. In these situations, stand your ground in a respectful manner while being open to their input and being able to recognize good ideas.

- **But be humble.** Make sure your ambition doesn't come across as arrogant. You may feel compelled to explain how you came to hold such a prominent position at such a young age, but bragging about your outstanding resume could backfire. 'Sometimes a leader is better off saying less,' says Sara Canaday, a leadership-development expert based in Austin, Texas. People who have been in a company longer are going to be hypersensitive to any signs of power and privilege. Don't make them hate you by repeatedly telling them who's boss.

---

[17]Lindsey Pollak, *Recalculating: Navigate Your Career Through the Changing World of Work*, Harper Business, 2021.

• **Learn from them.** Sometimes, what you don't know matters so much more than what you do.

   You are probably thinking: how can I be a leader if I have lesser experience? But, as a younger leader, that lack of experience might be your sweet spot. The most effective leaders will be able to tap into the expertise of others.

   There's a good chance some of the older people on the team have experience in an area you lack. As a young leader, you don't have to have all the answers. In fact, by being curious and seeking other's experience, it will have them wanting to help you rather than being an enemy. At the end of the day, you are in this position because of your potential, and one way to keep that trajectory going upwards is to have everyone on the team backing you.

• **Don't get too informal.** Limit talks about your social life. Stop harping about the party you went to or the romantic date that went terrible. Older workers, in particular, are used to working conditions where their personal lives aren't discussed as much. Maintain a professional demeanour, especially at first.

   Get to know them from a safe, healthy distance, though. Go to lunch, grab coffee or have a meet with this employee to learn more about them. Share what you're passionate about. Also ask them if they have any feedback for you and how you can be a more effective leader.

• **Show you are trying to understand them.** Clearly, there's an age gap as well as a lifestyle gap. Lifestyles are likely to be different from someone in their 40s or 50s to someone in their 20s or early 30s. Give your elder co-workers the respect they deserve because they may be a mother, father or simply have duties outside of work that differ from yours. Don't ridicule them for having 'no lives'. Even if it's jokingly, *just don't.* They might be struggling with balancing work life with a busy home life, and sometimes, we may not relate to these challenges because we may not be there yet in life.

- **Show you're mature enough to handle power.** One of the easiest ways to lose the respect of someone older than you is to act immature. There is absolutely no way around this other than to use the old saying, 'It's time to grow up fast.'

    The way you dress matters, the words you choose matter, what you do on the weekend matters, how you treat people matters, and what you share on social media matters. To net it out, *it all matters.* As a leader you are going to be judged, especially when you're young. With great power, comes great responsibility and the spotlight.

- Speak with a more senior leader to learn how they built their leadership style and what works for them.
- Experiment with several approaches in various situations, paying great attention to the output and how natural the style feels to you at the time. When it comes to modifying your strategy, be adaptable.
- Ask for feedback from both managers and colleagues. Although sometimes hard to hear, constructive feedback helps you grow into a successful leader.

- **Lastly, don't *show* them you're the leader.** 'Huh? How's that possible?' is what you're probably thinking. Let me show you. It's a natural instinct to not be immediately pleased by being told what to do by somebody who may be your granddaughter's age. Find a balance to be assertive and effective, while not over-communicating your authority. When having a hard conversation, don't resort to 'I'm-your-boss' type statements. These can come across as deadly to the older employees you're leading. Reinforce your credibility but manage your ego while doing so. Don't stretch the 'follow-me!' narrative.

Five Takeaways for You To Skim Through

- As a new-age leader, you have to recognize you won't lead a team of identical robots; they will all have different personalities and drivers.
- To lead introverts, you have to embrace their personality, give them space and also give them time to think before they can speak.
- For extroverts, let them shine amidst group projects. They create ideas by talking, so let them talk to other peers. Don't box them within their cabins.
- For older employees, you are to lead them with maturity, respect and empathy, unless you want to bruise their egos and leave a permanent bitter aftertaste.
- Don't make older employees feel ancient. Try to make them understand the ways of the modern world and technology. And of course, try to understand how their worlds worked—it'll make them love you.

5

MASTERING THE MILLENNIAL MANIA

Every generation brings something new to the workplace, and millennials are no exception. As a group, they tend to be highly educated, love to learn, and grew up with the Internet and digital tools in a way that can be highly useful when leveraged properly.[18]

—Kathryn Minshew, American entrepreneur, the CEO and co-founder of The Muse.

What comes to mind when you think about business or work? Suits, meetings, handshakes? Well, you can retire those old stereotypes. There are some fresh faces in the office. So, who's shaking things up? Millennials. And they represent the present and future of business.

'Millennials,' 'Generation Y,' 'Generation *WE*,' 'The Boomerang Generation,' 'The Peter Pan Generation'—they go by many names and were born roughly between 1980 and 2000.

---

[18]'PubTech Connect: Meet Kathryn Minshew, Sage of the Millennial Workforce', *Publishers Weekly*, 2 February 2017, https://www.publishersweekly.com/pw/by-topic/digital/conferences/article/72686-pubtech-connect-meet-kathryn-minshew-sage-of-the-millennial-workforce.html, Accessed on 2 March 2022.

There's no doubting that millennials are a source of intense debate: are they a blessing or a curse?

Managers and HR professionals frequently lament the difficulties they have in the workplace with younger employees, particularly millennials. But rather than being based on a fact, much of the dissatisfaction stems from assumptions about younger workers, partial truths and millennial mythology. Let's delve a little more into the millennial madness.

- **They are lovers of technology.** Millennials are a digital generation who have grown up with the Internet. Smartphones, tablets and laptops have revolutionized how they communicate and interact with one another and with the rest of the world. The generation is distinguished by characteristics like web savvy, curiosity, independence and tolerance. Millennials grew up in an electronic and online world, which fuelled their desire to learn new skills. They know how to use their smartphones, laptops and other technology devices to help them do their work better. The internet and cell phones are so important to this generation that they can't envisage a world without them.

- **They are *all* for social causes.** Because they grew up with the internet and social media, millennials bring their social awareness to work. Millennial employees are 79 per cent loyal to organizations that care about their social impact. Corporate social responsibility, they feel, is critical to eliminating poverty and enhancing life outcomes. They've encouraged their employees to volunteer their time, and numerous businesses have pledged to donate 1 per cent of their profits to charity.

- **Meaningful motivation over materialism and money.** Millennials want meaningful motivation. They can be described as people who are inspired by creative work, sharing their talents and making a difference in their communities. These inner motivators are frequently visible in how millennials approach their careers. Many people can regularly be found assisting others, inspiring others or striving to address a communal or global issue. Furthermore, many millennials want to set goals that allow them to advance their meaningful work rather than monetary advantages. While this generation's professional ambition typically aids advancement, many appear to do so for reasons other than a raise in income or monetary bonuses.

- **They adapt to survive.** Not only are millennials described as adaptive to change but many also embrace it. This generation has frequently been credited for ushering in advancements in business, technology and the economy. Most people appear to understand that these businesses are always evolving and that working practises in today's career field must evolve as well. This generation's ability to adapt to the constantly changing environment in which they live also allows them to grow and take on a range of occupations.

- **They think freely.** It could be due to the large availability of technology mediums, or the fact that millennials grew up amid the change from traditional to modernized and technologically sophisticated working techniques. Millennials may be more imaginative in their thinking as a result of this invention. When challenges develop at work, millennials are often able to come up with innovative methods to solve them.

- **They're progressive.** Millennials comprise the most ethnically diverse generation. After all, they were raised in a networked world. Through the usage of mobile apps and social media websites, they are connected. They are a digital generation that believes in technology; thus, they are optimistic about a sustainable future. Friendships are formed with people of many races, nationalities and genders. They are unafraid to advocate for diversity and inclusion at all levels of society.

By 2025, it's reported that millennials will make up 75 per cent of the workforce, effectively replacing baby boomers and drastically reducing the representation of Generation X. Millennials are no longer school and college-goers. They are not the future anymore. They are the present, and they have already taken over the workforce.

Instead of labelling millennials as flaky and unengaged (can we please do away with these types of biases?), it's time to give them what they want. To put it another way, let's properly mentor them as they rise to the top of the economy, leading with integrity and courage. However, our business culture, as defined by a competitive edge leftover from the 1980s, heavily influences what older generations perceive as 'flaky' and 'indecisive' behaviour. The majority of workers are no longer willing to work in such a harsh environment. So, rather than expecting people to fit into the culture, it's time for the culture to change.

The phrases 'entitled', 'lazy', 'narcissistic' and 'disloyal job-hoppers' are frequently used to describe the traits of millennials in the workplace. However, research suggests that at least when it comes to what millennials desire in a job, they aren't all that different from prior generations. If you focus on what matters to millennials, as a leader, you can create an environment where they can be both happy and productive.

What Do Millennials Want From Their Work?

1) **Sweet, Sweet, Freedom:** Millennials want to work when they want, where they want and how they want. They want the freedom to be their own boss with the guidance of a superior. They want to know they have agency over their lives.

2) **A Higher Purpose:** Gen Y is the generation that buys from and works for businesses that have a purpose at their core, and they want their core values to be aligned with their company's core values.

   A job is no longer just about a pay check; for millennials, it's very much about purpose, with 75 per cent saying they want their personal values to align with their company's values and are even willing to take a pay cut to work for a value-aligned company.

3) **A Fine Balance:** Work-life balance is a catchphrase among millennials, and many of them are succeeding in juggling their work and personal lives (or at least trying to).

   Employees are no longer required to be physically present at work every day for the majority of jobs. The traditional 9 to 5 work hours are starting to become an outdated concept. The technological shift to mobile communication has wholly redefined the work culture. On the one hand, technology has allowed millennials to work from anywhere. It has, on the other side, made youthful staff extremely approachable. They are 'always available' and don't mind working outside of normal business hours. Millennials are used to checking business emails on their phones during vacations and holidays. Flexible working choices such as work-from-home, telecommunication and remote working have made work-life harmony (however flawed) a reality.

4) **They Might Be Entitled, But Hardworking:** Millennials want to have a say and contribute their ideas. They resist doing repetitive or boring work. They desire a life outside of work, and they demand enough flexibility to be able to balance personal and professional obligations. But keep in mind that entitled does not imply slacker. Millennials put in long hours, don't expect their work to end when they leave the office and are highly driven. They want to do more than their job descriptions and advance in the company. Most significantly, millennials want to know that the work they do is valuable. They are willing to put in the effort (even long hours) if they believe they are serving a greater purpose.

5) **They Won't Settle for Less:** Millennials are a loyal group when a company does right by them. However, they wouldn't think twice about leaving a company if another one offers them a better opportunity to learn, grow or balance life and work. Remember, they have millions of options considering their qualifications and the internet. Do right or be abandoned.

6) **They Love Group Projects:** Whether it was soccer or ballet, most Millennial boys and girls participated in team sports, playgroups and other group activities as children. They value collaboration and seek out feedback and affirmation from others. Millennials are a truly no-one-left-behind generation, dedicated and loyal. They want to be a part of the process. The typical millennial employee does not prefer to work alone; instead, they prefer to collaborate with people in the firm, typically from other departments. Collaboration is a core value for millennials at work, and it would have been more difficult during the pandemic if it hadn't been for their familiarity with technology. Whether it's through

video conferencing or collaboration apps, millennials need to feel engaged and part of the team even if they are at home.

7) **They Want To Achieve:** Millennials have been nurtured and pampered by parents who didn't want to repeat the mistakes of the previous generation. They are self-assured, ambitious and goal-oriented. They also have high expectations of their bosses, seek out new challenges at work and aren't hesitant to oppose authority. Generation Y wants meaningful work and a clear path to success.

8) **They Want To Know What's Up:** Millennials have also left their mark on the way companies interact with their employees. Gone are the days when corporate communications were solely on a need-to-know basis. Millennials demand transparency from their bosses and want to know what's going on within the company. 'The relationship people have with companies has changed a lot over the years,' Christina Janzer, senior director of research and analytics at Slack, told Business News Daily. 'To have a successful relationship, you have to be very intentional about how you share what's happening and what's top of mind. There's a higher bar for that.'[19]

9) **They Want To Learn and Grow:** Millennials continue to learn even after they graduate from college. This group has a strong drive to learn and advance in their careers. They seek mentorship from people who have gone before them and value opportunities to learn more. Companies that offer opportunities for continued education and mentorship are

---

[19]Donna Fuscaldo, 'Managing Millennials in the Workplace', Business News Daily, 19 November 2021, https://www.businessnewsdaily.com/15974-millennials-in-the-workplace.html, Accessed on 2 March 2022.

more likely to retain millennial employees than those that do not.

10) **They Want a Diverse Workplace:** Millennials embody what it means to be a global citizen. Because they are more socially conscious, they acknowledge, encourage, recognize and respect variety. Social media has brought the entire world closer in ways that previous generations could not have imagined. As a result, millennials are the most culturally and racially diverse generation in history. 67 per cent of job searchers consider diversity when evaluating organizations and employment offers, according to Glassdoor. Their attitude toward diversity differs significantly from that of past generations. They define diversity as the introduction of fresh ideas, points of view and experiences. Millennials are not only accepting of diversity, but also passionate about it. They feel that diversity in the workplace is critical, whether in terms of race, colour, demographics or equal representation. Diversity and inclusion programmes in the workplace are likely to skyrocket in the coming years. Millennials have grown up in a social networking world that is hyper-connected. Their way of life is around socialization. They have an innate need to share their thoughts and ideas, and they want a similar working environment.

11) **They Crave Rawness:** Millennials gravitate toward companies that adopt a relatable, straightforward communication style. They've been exposed to so much advertising throughout their lives that they're sick of corporate jargon and meaningless buzzwords. They just want you to keep it real.

12) **They Want To Do Good and Do Well:** Do millennials want to save the world? Yes. However, doing good does not take precedence over doing well. Millennials in the workplace desire jobs that allow them to make a positive contribution

to society while also rewarding them appropriately. One does not take the place of the other.

> - If you want to be a cutting-edge leader, be a decent corporate citizen.
> - Make sure millennials understand how their work directly contributes to your company's positive effect. Corporate social responsibility activities are particularly important to younger workers.
> - They should be compensated fairly. Workplace millennials are aware of typical salary, so don't try to keep wage information from them.

What Do These Multiform Millennials Expect From You As Their Next-Gen Leader?

- **They want you to understand their wants.** There was once a strong sense in the business world that if you didn't absolutely need something, you didn't ask for it. This 'don't complain unless you have to' attitude may be a method of staying out of trouble and keeping your job, but it doesn't do your staff or your organization any favours. Millennials strongly believe that their needs matter, and they aren't afraid to speak up. Perhaps they need more time to finish a project or could use a personal day. Unlike previous generations of workers, millennials will let you know where they stand.
- **They want to be the next next-gen leader like you.** According to a survey, 91 per cent of respondents expressed a desire to lead. Nearly 50 per cent of them also said that they believed leadership is important to them.

  Millennials often equate leadership with empowerment. They have extreme opinions on most matters, and they like to take charge of things. They also show a high inclination towards leadership skills such as communication, relationship building, problem-solving and decision making.

Employers must focus on developing future leaders rather than just productive employees when engaging millennials in the workforce. Modelling and mentoring leadership abilities early on is the best method to build leaders among millennials.

- Check in with them on a regular basis to see how they're doing. Provide them with mentors and comments on a regular basis.
- Be there for support when things get tough.
- Give them as much control as possible. Micromanaging isn't a good idea.

- **They are *both* needy and independent.** Millennials need to feel like what they are doing is important and that they are on the right track. Yes, it sounds a little needy (and it is). But many millennials grew up with constant praise from their baby boomer parents. It's what they know.

  Younger workers are frequently chastised for being needy, clinging to their parents and constantly seeking praise and favour. While millennials demand help, feedback, mentoring and to be acknowledged in the job, this does not make them a dependent. They are, in fact, being very strategic. They consider what they require to be successful, and they ask for it.

- **They want a seat at your table.** Millennials, regardless of their status within an organization, grew up having a say in family decisions and expect the same at work. They want to be heard, and they value the firms that allow them to do so. It may be difficult for a baby boomer or Generation X leader to accept this, but you must adapt; millennials are ambitious. Give millennials the road and the rules, and they'll work hard to fulfil their own and the company's objectives.

- **The long-run.** Among millennials who admired their managers, words like 'growth' and 'development' came up often. Whereas previous generations praised effective leaders for being 'engaging', 'smart' and 'strategic', millennials praised managers who had their 'best interests' at heart—especially in terms of their long-term professional and personal development.

- **Honesty is the best policy.** Millennials want to feel like they have an open and honest relationship with their manager and co-workers and that there won't be any nasty surprises when they join a company. Once they've signed on, they want assurance that their opinion is valued and both give and receive a good deal of feedback. Managers who are seen to be saving the day and showering themselves in glory are not celebrated by this generation. Instead, millennials appreciate it when leaders let them be the hero by giving them the tools to reach their full potential.

- **They don't want *you* solving their issues; they want *your help* such that they can solve their *own* issues.** When millennials described how their managers helped them in problematic situations, the word 'empathetic' was mentioned most often. Unlike Gen X, who wants someone who can come in and solve a problem, millennials want moral support and understanding to help them work through the problem themselves.

- **They want both technology and human interaction.** Millennials are accustomed to using technology. They've known it since they were children, and it's been ingrained in their friendships and daily activities. Millennials appreciate technology at work because it helps them save time and minimizes drudgery. But just because kids spend so much time glued to their phones doesn't mean they don't need other people. In reality, millennials' organizational commitment, job satisfaction, engagement and retention are all influenced by their sense of belonging at work.

- Allow millennials to support their job with their preferred technology.
- Consider establishing reverse mentorship programmes so that your digital attuned millennials may assist more seasoned but less tech-savvy employees.
- Meet with them in person as often as you can, especially when it comes to remuneration, growth or performance.

How Do You, as a Cutting-Edge Leader, Master Millennials?

- **Lead with an out-of-the-box mindset.** Millennials praised executives that lead with an internal compass, as opposed to Gen Z, who identified their ideal leader as embodying the company's ideals. Millennials look up to managers that lead with a 'unique mindset'—a word that was repeated in the survey answers that highlighted leadership values—rather than mimicking the company's external ideals.
- **Shine online.** If your company isn't employing social media effectively, millennials will think you're irrelevant (sorry, it also turns out subtlety isn't their strength). Keep your social media outlets active at all times. This doesn't mean constantly posting jobs or product updates. Try to start conversations that will engage your audience. Talk about

topics that relate to your company or will interest your followers. It is suggested to allow your Millennial employees to help you with your social media strategy. After all, they are the experts.

- **Rope them in.** Everyone wants to be a part of making decisions that affect them. This encounter, however, is especially profound for millennials. When they feel involved, they're 4 to 64 times more likely to give extra, stay longer, recommend their workplace and contribute their best to their workplace.

- **Tickle their challenge-buds.** To keep your millennial employees engaged and invested in their jobs, organizations must create interesting and challenging opportunities. Millennials are very adept at using technology. They don't regard learning new computer languages or gaining new abilities as a difficult task. To stay employable in the future, 74 per cent of millennials are willing to learn new skills or retrain. Millennials prefer occupations that offer some level of challenge to those that are boring and monotonous. As a result, certain job roles that have become common in recent time didn't even exist a decade ago.

- **Make them trust you, and they're yours forever.** Some questions are difficult to respond to. Those, on the other hand, are the ones that build or break an employee's faith and trust in their boss. Mistakes and misunderstandings occur despite the best intentions and efforts. The only way to deal with problems is to be honest and listen to all inputs so you can figure out where the breaks are occurring and address them head on. Millennial employees feel their leaders are deeply trustworthy when they are truthful in difficult situations, whether or not they get the answer they were hoping for.

- **Don't even try breaking their beloved balance.** Make it clear that your organization values a healthy work-life balance. Inform them about sponsored events outside of the workplace, employee benefits, charity and volunteer work, and any fitness or health-related programmes you offer. You can also tell them that their time-in/time-out is up to them as long as they accomplish deadlines, goals and attend meetings. Allow them to work from home on occasion if at all possible. Reduce work-life balance and overload—these are real challenges that will push millennials away.

- **Get real or get lost (Harsh, but being real here.)** Cut the jargon. Banish corporate speak from your job descriptions and employer brand content, and focus on speaking like a normal person. You don't need to try and adopt 'millennial speak'—honestly, it's probably better to avoid it at all costs, because content that feels inauthentic is worse than content that's dry and dated. Just use simple, succinct language that anyone can relate to and you'll spark up real conversations in no time at all.

- **The perfect blend of personal and professional.** Don't assume you need to text millennials a message rife with emojis to effectively communicate with them. Most millennials prefer a manager who communicates in a way that is transparent and direct but also knows when it's okay to not be so starchy and buttoned-up. In written communication, replace formal salutations with casual greetings. With face-to-face communication, don't be afraid to let your guard down and connect with your report about shared interest. The more that you can be authentically yourself while also keeping it professional, the more likely the message you're trying to convey will be heard.

- **Let them fail.** Along with innovation comes the ability to test new ideas and make big bets. Millennials want to work for a company that encourages them to take risks and either reap the benefits or learn from their mistakes. Failure is viewed as the enemy since no one celebrates your failures. In actuality, failure is a normal part of the learning process as long as we don't fail in the same way twice. Managers who promote failure and lead them through the process of learning from it are sought after by millennials.

- **Give authentic feedback.** Millennials are a smarter generation and they can see through both fake compliments and criticism. When they perform a task, they expect their leader to critically analyse it and provide them with constructive feedback. Sugar-coating doesn't work for them; yet, they would want their leaders to be polite and friendly. The trick is to strike a balance and provide them with a real response. Start the conversation with the positive aspects and then, move on to the improvement areas. Do not use harsh words but suggest a better way of doing things. You could also cite your own experiences to make things more relatable.

- **Stroke their egos (not all the time, of course.)** Do not depend upon organizational level recognition. A single word of praise in team meetings, a congratulatory e-mail and a pat on the back goes a long way to appreciating someone's efforts.

- **Lead through collaboration.** The traditional top-down management style doesn't work for millennials, who prefer to collaborate with teams and often consider their leaders more as the team captain rather than the owner. When leading millennials, remember that even though you lead the team, you're also one of the key players. The cutting-edge next-gen leader knows that they have as much to learn from their employees as they have to teach. As you develop your millennial team members, keep the lines of communication open. You may be surprised at what you learn as well.

- **Respect ideas, not hierarchy.** Great companies are run by ideas and not hierarchy. If you are the type of boss that wants millennials to work with a fresh mind, then you have to give them an open platform to share and discuss ideas. Being their leader, you must ensure that they are:

- Receiving enough support to speak up and perform.
- Given a chance to implement and execute their ideas.
- Able to measure the outcome of their projects or campaigns.
- Constantly motivated with good ideas by the leadership.

Asking them to follow your ideas only because you come with a lot of experience might not be the best way to settle a conversation. This is one situation where numbers don't bother them. Give them a reason why you may or may not want to go ahead with their plan, strategy or idea. If it makes sense to them, they will agree with you, understand the issue and learn from you for future reference.

- **Be *all* about variety.** Emphasize your company's commitment to diversity and inclusion across all your employer branding channels. However, don't be scared to admit where you're lacking. Recognizing that you still have work to do and demonstrating that you're making progress helps millennial candidates trust you by demonstrating that you take the issue as seriously as they do.

- **Tell them *why* rather than *how*.** Ask a millennial to jump, and he'll ask—why. Why, you ask? Millennials were raised by democratic baby boomer parents who asked for their opinions on everything from which new TV to buy to where to go on vacation. They also grew up with the virtual soapbox that is social media. These two conditions combined have made for a generation that values the opportunity to give their opinions. Once they've given their opinion or idea, they want to understand why it's being either accepted or rejected. Don't be afraid to tell a millennial 'no', but prepare to back it up with the reasoning behind it. It is said that leadership is the art of getting someone else to do something you want to be done because he wants to do it. When leading millennials, don't just assign them work 'because you said so'. Get them on board by being transparent about why each job matters.

- **Make them believe.** In a recent Twitter discussion on millennial issues, @throwingwords concisely put it this way: 'Provide purpose and promote passion. The 'why' matters more than "what".'[20] Yes indeed. It's quite easy for employees in large organizations (I worked in diverse financial services for decades and well understand this) to feel terribly removed from consumers and the core of the firm. It is the responsibility of effective management to 'paint the big picture' and explain how an employee's position fits into the larger picture—and why it matters.

- **Don't be a killjoy.** In earlier work cultures, stern behaviour was often equated with determination, gravity and leadership skill. However, negative outlooks are no longer embraced by the merry-making millennials. They prefer to view the world with a sense of optimism, and they often look to CEOs and managers as role models for positivity. They also value humour and quick wit since they grew up with memes and

---

[20]Victor Lipman, 'The Best Concise Description Of How To Manage Millennials', *Forbes*, 15 June 2016, https://www.forbes.com/sites/victorlipman/2016/06/15/the-best-concise-description-of-how-to-manage-millennials/?sh=575b663d4605, Accessed on 2 March 2022.

stand-up comics, after all. As a cutting-edge next-gen leader, rely on puns, sarcasm and jokes to underscore your points and relieve the tension of long workdays. Your millennials are more likely to react positively even if you approach serious topics with some good old comedy.

Here Are Some Extra Don'ts You Can Follow To Ride the Millennial Mania Like a Boss

- **Don't be vague.** Removing novelty buzzwords like 'ninja' and 'guru' from your hiring process is the first step (they can see straight through the nonsense), and once you've found your new hire, making sure they have a clear route of progression—vertically or horizontally—is the way to keep them from crossing you out.
- **Don't be an autocrat, be a pal.** Groomed by social media, there's a strong part of the millennial psyche that strives to befriend everyone. Don't take this as an invitation to relinquish your control; they value a competent, fair and inspiring leader above all else. Instead of seeking personal appreciation, concentrate on obtaining their professional regard.
- **Don't misunderstand their motivators.** Ping pong tables and free beer on tap may be a way to showcase a cool and relaxed work environment, but it's not impressing the millennial generation very much—if at all—especially long term.

It's not about the bells and whistles for attracting (and retaining) millennial employees. According to *Forbes*, when you take a deeper look into the millennial generation, what they want is quite simple: a sense of purpose, ability to provide value, appreciation and a good working atmosphere.[21]

---

[21]Ibid.

- **Don't hover around them all the time.** Pesky micromanagement doesn't work too well for anyone, and even less well for this generation. This doesn't mean you lose your power. Management needs to get results—just as it always has. But *how* those results are attained matters. A lot.
- **Don't shrug them off.** You won't be purposely undermined or usurped by a millennial since they understand that it's your duty to be the boss. They have, however, grown up with extremely attentive parents and the continual, worldwide platform of the internet, so they have a strong opinion and demand to be heard. On the plus side, most millennials have their finger on the pulse and are ready to usher your company into the twenty-first century.

Five Takeaways for You To Skim Through:

- Millennials are the present and future of the workplace; they are the largest generation in today's workforce. Today's cutting-edge leader knows he/she needs them to build the modern business empire.
- Millennials are digital pioneers. They have seen technology transform the world, and so, they're lovers of gadgets.
- Millennials don't run after money; they want meaning. Tell them why they're working for you and why their work matters, and they will never leave you.
- Millennials love some good old praise—recognize and appreciate them.
- Millennials hate being micro-managed or yelled at. They want a seat at your table and be treated as equals, irrespective of what their positions are.

6

THE GEN Z FRENZY

Generation Z has arrived - and they're very
different from millennials... They want to work.
They want to do a very good job at that position.
They are not looking at climbing the ranks quickly.
They are looking at getting value quickly.[22]

—Denise Villa, Founder, The Center
for Generational Kinetics

Look up 'millennials' on Google and see what comes up. Prepare for an avalanche of search results, because millennials are the most talked-about generation since, well, ever. Their time in the limelight isn't about to end anytime soon, though.

But an even greater demographic is going to burst onto the scene, and this group is about to have a huge impact on the workplace. Millennials may currently be the largest generation, but with Gen Z projected to overtake millennials as the most

---

[22]Team CGK, 'WHAT DOES GEN Z VALUE IN THE WORKPLACE?', The Center for Generational Kinetics, https://genhq.com/what-does-gen-z-value-in-the-workplace/, Accessed on 2 March 2022.

populous, they will one day rule a workforce that will look very different.

So, what is Gen Z, exactly? People born between 1996 and the early 2000s are included in this category. As a result, a big portion of them are currently in college or are just starting out in the workforce. That suggests you'll be seeing them as co-workers or employees in the near future. Also, be aware! They're not like millennials at all. It is only a next-gen, cutting-edge leader who will be well-prepared for this future Gen Z frenzy in the workplace. The cutting-edge leader knows well, how the Gen Z think, and leads them without actually 'leading' them (if you know what I mean.)

Gen Z is young, which means there's still a lot to learn about what makes them tick. However, when we learn more about them, we find that they have a growing number of differences from millennials. Many people think of Gen Z as millennials 2.0, but they're completely wrong. They've been reared differently, have a different relationship with technology, a different perspective on money and have grown up at a different time than millennials.

The Gen Z generation, like the millennials before them, has grown up with technology literally at their fingertips as they prepare to graduate from high school or college and begin their first adult jobs. This generation has never known a world without the internet or, in certain cases, smartphones. So naturally, they do share traits (which is why they're always clubbed together.) What are some common traits?

- A desire to find (or create) meaning.
- A deep connection with technology.
- A motivation to contribute to the world.

- Being highly educated.
- Cultural diversity.
- A desire for their own personalized experience.
- A *need* for work-life balance.
- Progressive thinking.

To be honest, and not to put down the magical millennials, Gen Z is perhaps the most informed, responsible and hip of all the generations. So, for their sake, don't mix up millennials and Generation Z. While they share similar characteristics, they come from distinct generations for *a purpose*.

Gen Z workers have got their millennial bosses shaking in their boots, unless these millennial bosses are new-age leaders like you will be after having read this book. Older generations fear Gen Zers, who demand a better work-life balance with confidence and assertiveness. The TikTok generation delegated authority to their leaders, isn't afraid to request mental health days, works less after completing daily duties and sets their own hours. Millennials paved the way for a change in better flexibility and wellbeing at work, but Gen Z is turning it from a workplace perk to workplace norm.

A leader who isn't cutting edge makes a mistake of conveniently clubbing Gen Z and millennials together. We aren't going to do that here.

Millennials versus Gen Z:

Millennials	Generation Z
When it comes to making decisions, millennials have a more optimistic mindset than risk-averse Gen Z.	Generation Z may lean more toward security and money. This is a pragmatic age; they want to make a difference, but their primary motivation is to have a stable life outside of work. If you're hoping to hire Generation Z, you might be able to entice them with promises of employment security and future promotions.
Millennials are comparatively more focused on doing one task considering they've spent a few years without smartphones and Wi-Fi (fortunately or unfortunately.) Younger millennials grew up with some of the same technology used by Gen Z, but it was much less pervasive.	If you thought your millennial employees were easily distracted, always flipping between texts and emails, just wait until you start working with members of Gen Z. These young people have always lived in a connected world and are accustomed to receiving regular updates from a variety of apps. It comes easy to them to switch between tasks and pay attention to a variety of stimuli at the same time.
Millennials tend to value teamwork and input from others more highly qualified. They like to share their workspace with others and be socially engaged with their co-workers—thriving in open office plans.	Members of Gen Z are more independent and can prefer to figure things out themselves. They are more competitive and focused on their own success, desiring to have complete control over the final output of their labour.

	While Gen Z does not have a difficulty working in a group setting, many young people prefer to work on their own projects as much as possible. Gen Zers can prove themselves to companies by working independently and showcasing their talents and abilities.
Millennials may take longer to grasp new internet tools but are still eager to learn and enjoy knowing how and why web features work.	Millennials have adapted to a tech-driven lifestyle while Gen Z was raised in it. Gen Zers are known as the first generation of 'digital natives,' meaning that they learned, made friendships and grew up online. They have an almost incredible grasp of how to utilize and exploit the internet to achieve their objectives, and they are well-prepared to keep up with technological advancements.
Millennials rely on digital communication tools and platforms.	Despite being dubbed 'digital natives', Gen Zers, in contrast, actually show a preference for face-to-face communication. I don't blame them—they're sick and tired of everyday birthday video calls, virtual dates and online classes after the pandemic.

Millennials see their career as the most important thing in their life, although they do seek a balance between the professional and personal.	For Gen Zers, their career is merely a part of their life, and so, their desire for work-life balance is stronger. 'Gen Z won't put up with our corporate BS,' says Tim Sackett, Society for Human Resources Management Senior Certified Professional, HRU Technical Resources. 'If you say, "Well, the CEO starts work every day at 7 a.m. and works until 8 p.m., and you should, too!" they'll say, "That works for Mary, but it doesn't work for me!"'[*]

- Gen Zs are pragmatic, millennials are idealistic.
- Millennials search for meaning in their work, whilst Gen Z prioritize job security and pay.
- Gen Z values autonomy, whilst millennials thrive on collaboration.
- While millennials were digital pioneers, Gen Z is a digital native.
- Millennials want to work in a variety of jobs, whereas Gen Z wants to work in a variety of fields.
- Gen Z prefers face-to-face conversation over digital communication, whereas millennials prefer the opposite.
- Gen Z places a higher importance on socially aware businesses than millennials. Generation Z mobilizes for a number of causes, ranging from social to environmental concerns. They refuse to accept traditional gender roles and

[*]Dana Wilkie, 'Generation Z Says They Work the Hardest, But Only When They Want To', SHRM, 11 June 2019, https://www.shrm.org/resourcesandtools/hr-topics/employee-relations/pages/gen-z-worries-about-work-skills.aspx, Accessed on 2 March 2022.

will combat racial and sexual prejudice with zeal. They're also more likely to seek out organizations that promote workplace diversity and equality.

In What Ways Can the Gen Z Surpass Millennials? (Not Trying To Start a War Here)

- **Tech-savviness makes them more adaptable.** Even though millennials are tech-literate and able to embrace the winds of change, there's no denying that while they grew up with dial-up Internet, Myspace and AOL, that's a hugely different experience to Facebook and Google.

  Gen Z has grown up, and their entire lives are even being documented as we speak on social media, either by themselves or by their parents. The world is smaller, technology is faster and the world exists largely on a screen. This may sound bad, but Gen Z has better virtual communication skills, online collaboration skills and a more entrepreneurial spirit as a result of this: they're used to figuring things out for themselves. Think about how fast these Gen Zers adapted to e-learning, e-working and new applications during the pandemic.

- **Better at juggling between multiple tasks.** Though Gen Z can be less focused than their millennial counterparts, in school or college, they will create a document on their school computer, do research on their phone or tablet, while taking notes on a notepad, then finish in front of the TV with a laptop, while face-timing a friend—you get the picture.

  Gen Z can quickly and efficiently shift between work and play, with multiple distractions going on in the background—working on multiple tasks at once. Talk about multi-multi-tasking. Just think about how this kind of flow might reshape the office.

- **A more global mindset.** Millennials were considered the first 'global' generation with the development of the internet, but as more of the world comes online, Generation Z will become more global in their thinking, interactions and relatability. Diversity will be an expectation of Generation Z. Due to this global mindset, Gen Zers can cater to a wider audience, better understand consumer behaviours and hence, help their leaders understand the global market better. They're the most rampant consumers themselves, remember?

- **Natural E-learners.** They're natural gatherers of information and self-learners. YouTube, Wikipedia and e-How have all grown up with them. They know how to find the knowledge they need and aren't hesitant to use their resources. Consider Buzzfeed. Young people frequent this news site since the articles are brief and visually appealing.

- **Early beginners.** Many business leaders are predicting that more teens, between the ages of 16 and 18 will go straight into the workforce, opting out of the traditional route of higher education and instead finishing school online—if at all. Would you make a significant investment, potentially resulting in years of debt, knowing that new, more affordable (not to mention handier) internet options are appearing every day?

  Gen Z understands the genuine importance of autonomy, and knowledge is no exception. You can bet that if a Gen Zer believes they are capable of learning anything at an early age or by a more efficient, non-traditional way, they will seize the opportunity.

- **Need for speed.** Generation Z were born into the brave new world of technology, and it really has shaped the way they operate on a daily basis. They can tweet faster than they can speak, type faster than they can write, and like a status faster than they can applaud. Because of the digital landscape, they are capable of accomplishing numerous jobs at once, making them effective all-rounders in the workplace. After all, you're dealing with a generation that shops, dates, learns and works all in a matter of seconds.

- **They mean business, *literally.*** Because of the vast technological tools at their fingertips, Gen Z feels empowered to act independently. They do not have to wait for someone to give them an opportunity to make money, learn, create or connect. They can record videos, create music, start businesses and connect with people around the world with the resources on their devices. As a result, they are incredibly entrepreneurial. Online shopping sites and social media marketing has shown them that anyone can start a business *anytime, anywhere and at any age*.

  A cutting-edge leader taps the pragmatic, entrepreneurial spirit of their Gen Z team members so that their business flourishes.

- **More individuality means more creativity.** 92 per cent of Generation Z have a digital footprint. The likes of Instagram, Facebook and Snapchat all facilitate a desire to be individual. This portrayal of uniqueness is an inherent feature of Gen Z candidates, which is a big advantage in many industries—most notably within the creative sectors. Many firms' personal brands are becoming a major driving force, with their employees proving to be increasingly powerful with customers. Individuality can flourish in this environment. And this individuality, when pooled together at the workplace, leads to better ideas, innovation and synergy.

And of Course, What Are Some Major Gen Z Cons?

- Career impatience and job-hopping.
- Shorter attention spans. They're easily distracted.
- Poor mental health (especially after the pandemic.)
- Some of them might be a little too privileged and entitled.
- Internet addicts. You see it all around you.
- Demanding, both professionally and personally.
- Over-reliance on technology, be it devices or the world wide web.
- Unpredictable.

How Do You Charm These Young Powerhouses as a Cutting-Edge Leader?

- **Be clear as a crystal.** Honesty is part of the deal when it comes to creating an authentic atmosphere. And, whether at work or at home, honesty is the foundation of any good connection. I don't believe that a desire for transparency is unique to Generation Z. Even though it's uncomfortable, most people want to hear the truth. However, when it comes to the workplace, Gen Z may be the first to demand it from management.

  My younger cousin Sasha told me she still remembers sitting for an online meeting in March 2020 as the COVID-19 pandemic began. Her Gen Z co-workers were worried since they didn't know what would happen to them. They'd never worked from home before, and that was the last thing on their minds. They were more concerned about whether or not they would have a job next week.

  Sasha's boss Cody pulled groups of his employees into meetings so that they could air concerns and figure out what their plan was. Ultimately, only a few of them were enabled to work from home because no one knew what they were getting themselves into. People were upset, and they had a right to be, they were going into their spring break without a job and weren't sure when they'd get it back, if at all.

However, Cody was the person who held the entire team together through his dedication to transparency in times of crisis. He obtained everyone's phone numbers and made sure to stay in touch. He made everyone on the team feel welcome and important. He kept them up to speed on what he was hearing and didn't try to deceive them. If he knew something, so did the rest of the crew. Because of the way Cody treated the team during a difficult moment, the team had a better relationship with him after they fully converted to working from home. His openness aided a group of Gen Z workers in navigating an unexpected situation. That's a true forward-thinking leader. Generation Zers expect their leaders to be open and honest about what they know and don't know. That honesty should pertain to conversations about returning to the office or simply being straightforward about the time commitment of an expedited project.

- **They thrive in a high-tech environment**. Your typical Gen Z kid was in computer class as early as first grade being taught the Microsoft suite. He learned how to type in middle school using orange typing covers that hid the letters on the keys, he learned how to date by chatting on Facebook, he learned how to Google anything, anytime, anywhere.

  Now, on average, Gen Z will multi-task across at least five screens. Gen Z has stronger virtual communication skills and online collaboration skills compared to previous generations. The cutting-edge leader can use this generation's digital skillset to their advantage if they surround their Gen

Z employees with high-tech environments.

Employees can be given laptops, tablets and cell phones, and the workstation can be surrounded by digital monitors and virtual reality. Digital programmes that can improve workflow are also familiar to Gen Z. Leaders may use this generation's talents in platforms like Vidyard and Slack to boost workplace communication, as well as cloud systems like Google Drive, Microsoft's OneDrive and Dropbox.

- **And with a high-speed leader.** In an age of access, digital fluency and the desire to make an impact, Gen Zers have been made impatient; they expect things to happen instantly. To meet these expectations, leaders must adapt their decision-making processes and provide information at a faster pace. They must be ready to process data at the same speed as Gen Z employees and provide answers in real time.

  The cutting-edge leader understands and appreciates generational differences and the need for a different style of leadership when working with Gen Zers. Leaders must be instantaneously available and digitally aware now and in the future to keep their teams motivated. They must demonstrate a commitment to their employees' development and be actively involved in the race to have a positive impact on the world.

- **Mental health first, pay-check next.** Despite the fact that these young powerhouses are ambitious and want to make a lot of money, studies show that they prefer employment that allow them to live a healthy and quiet lifestyle, even if the pay isn't as good. Give them a fun and interesting job to do and they'll go above and beyond.

  These young professionals are eager to work extra hours and overtime if they are compensated for it. They want to be judged on their own merits because they are competitive.

Remember, don't try to own their work—these guys own their careers.

- **Give them some good old face-to-face interaction.** While you're a cutting-edge leader and they're the new-age workers, you both cannot deny the power of an old-school, face-to-face conversation at work. Your Gen Z workers may need less training on technology; however, they may require more in offline interpersonal communication. Think about it, the poor souls have been boxed within their homes on their phones and laptops—especially after COVID-19. The empathetic new-age leader brings them out of their pandemic shells and talks to them one-on-one.

  These Gen Zers are also used to freely expressing their opinions online, so make sure you encourage collaboration between them through group discussions, open houses, lunch meetings and in-person Q&A sessions.

- **They want to hear from you frequently.** Receiving feedback from supervisors isn't a new idea. Although, Gen Z differs in both how and how often they prefer to receive feedback. To better connect to their younger Gen Z reports, leaders can try delivering feedback in-person instead of using other digital channels, such as email or chat.

  On a frequent basis, Gen Z wants to hear from their leaders. 60 per cent of Gen Zers expect several check-ins from their employer over the week, and 40 per cent of them want such encounters to happen daily or multiple times a day. To provide feedback, the new-age leader can schedule daily, weekly or bi-weekly check-ins with their younger subordinates.

  Interactions as short as 15 minutes or even 10 minutes can create long-lasting work relationships and timeless dedication.

- **Let them use their brains.** Gen Zers possess a unique point of view regarding everything they come across and *they know it*. Being born and brought up amidst technological advancements, they always think ahead while taking any major step.

  Many old-school leaders often make the mistake of neglecting their ideas owing to their young age and inexperience. However, the same could help your business thrive in the long run and stay competitive. The Gen Z youngsters are constantly flooded with the latest information from around the world. This thing, combined with their high enthusiasm, gives them an ample opportunity to come up with out-of-the-box solutions to various problems. I don't see why the next-gen leader wouldn't use that to his/her advantage.

- **Give them the best of *all* worlds.** These are individuals who have infinite options on the internet on what to buy, what to order for dinner, who to romance, what café to go to with friends, what to learn, what movie to stream on date-night or what job to pick. What makes you think they'd settle for one monotonous task at work?

  Gen Zers have perfected the ability of multitasking and paying attention to multiple tasks at the same time. They can be hyper-focused because to their short attention span, which allows them to acquire new information rapidly and successfully respond to the dynamic change. In today's corporate world, where variables are continuously changing and one must remain on top of current trends to maintain a competitive advantage, Gen Zers' capacity to multitask is a big benefit. Let them dip their toes in multiple fields—communication, content creation, marketing, sales—you name it.

- **A sprinkle of healthy competition.** Millennials may have been the generation of open floor plans and the 'we're all in this together' mentality, but Gen Z works differently because they consider themselves to be highly individualized workers.

  I had a word with my niece Lara, who's 21. She told me, despite the benefits of collaboration, she knew working with her friends or classmates in the library decreased her pace and productivity. If Lara wanted an assignment done efficiently, she had to do it by herself—within her own space. And Lara is not alone with this thinking, as research shows 69 per cent of Gen Z youngsters prefer their own workspace.

  Leaders who want to see their Gen Z employees do their best work should provide opportunities for them to get away from the congested office. Provide locations where employees can take turns using a shared office space if your company has an open floor plan, or offer a mix of in-office and work-from-home options. Additionally, you can increase their productivity through some healthy competition and incentives. Gen Z is motivated by experiential rewards and badges, similar to those used within competitive gaming—think Counter Strike, Fortnite, Overwatch or PUBG (just without the violence, of course.) Just the way of winning in these games gives you an instant rush or boost, the Gen Zs need motivation through rewards and recognition.

- **They want you to care.** The new-age leader must take an active interest in getting to know their Gen Z employees. Understanding one's story, needs, wants and desires extends the human dignity that Gen Z deserves, craves and longs for at work.

  'Ugh! It's messy,' you may think, but rich relationships are a cornerstone of living well and working well. 'But it's also very time consuming.' Yes, but so is constantly hiring and training new talent to replace peers who abandoned you. 'Personal emotions aren't for the workplace.' Now, that right there, is classic outdated thinking. Get rid of it. As work and life continue to blend more and more, managing the whole-self of your workers will be the new norm. Caring for others isn't beneath any leader at any level. Make your Gen Z gems feel known.

- **Go remote or go home**. Yes, let them stay home at times and they'll remain loyal to you, always. Of the groups that seem most primed to work remotely indefinitely, Gen Z leads the pack. They're digital natives who intuitively grasp new productivity tools; it's natural for younger workers to connect via DMs or video chat, for example, technologies that some older workers have struggled to grasp. Working from home—or other remote locations—appears to be an obvious option for this group. Just like their hybrid personalities and the hybrid world they have been born in, these young powerhouses want hybrid work.

Mark Thompson, American author and Head of Growth at The Happiness Index, believes that, contrary to popular belief, hybrid teams are closer teams. He explains, 'Personally, I feel so much closer to my team than I ever did before, even though I see them in-person less. Getting to know everyone on a personal level with flatmates roaming in the background, dogs barking on calls, kids screaming for attention. That sense of connection, has for THI [The Happiness Index] at least, led to a stronger more collective culture—we were all in the bunker together.'[23]

[23]Elle Whitehead-Smith, 'The Challenges of Modern Leadership – What Does the Future Hold For Leaders?', The Happiness Index, 14 July 2021, https://

A recent study by Slack found that flexibility is a key reason why employees are attracted to the hybrid work model. Finding the precious work-life balance is easier for workers when their work is flexible. When your Gen Z workers have control of their work schedules, they can free up time to take care of the things that crop up in their personal lives—whether it's running an errand, picking up younger siblings from day-care or being home for a delivery. Some of the other advantages of hybrid work include:

- Increased productivity due to flexibility.
- Saved time and energy due to not having to travel to the office for work.
- Being free to work when and where one pleases has a significant positive impact on employee satisfaction.
- Being able to dress casually, cook more and spend time with loved ones all contribute to this boost in your peers' mental health.
- Reduced office costs—electricity, assigned desks and all the other factors can be avoided as your workers work from home.
- However, since only work-from-home can lead to loneliness, isolation and unchecked progress, a hybrid work schedule also creates scope for coming to office and avoiding the domestic distractions (yes, I'm talking crying babies, ringing doorbells and chatty nannies.)

thehappinessindex.com/blog/modern-leadership-challenges/, Accessed on 3 March 2022.

How Do You Communicate With Gen Zers (Without Trying Hard or Cracking Dad-Jokes?)

- **Using visuals can be even more effective.** A study found that, compared to millennials, Gen Z spends more time consuming visual and video media, and is more likely to share visual content on social media. As the cliché goes: a picture is worth a thousand words. Know the value of emojis, stickers, GIFs, memes, videos or playlists. Dry e-mails and angry texts will put these youngsters off. However, don't overdo the emojis and memes.
- **Pop-cultural references can never go wrong.** A new song that's gone viral? Hum it occasionally. A new movie on Netflix that's taken the world by storm? Tell your employees what you think about it. A new meme that's been all over Twitter? Casually include it in conversations. They're going to fall in love with you, I promise. Why? Because you're relatable to them.
- **Try to take it offline.** Gen Zs tend to blur the line between work and life outside of work. 'They want buddies and friends, which goes against everything you're taught in management class,' Heather Watson, behavioural designer at The Center for Generational Kinetics, told CNBC. 'They want to be socially connected with everyone. They want to be socially connected with their boss as well' and for that, the new-age leader needs to communicate face-to-face, pleasantly.'[24]

---

[24]Chris Morris, '61 million Gen Zers are about to enter the US workforce and radically change it forever', CNBC, 2 May 2018, https://www.cnbc.com/2018/05/01/61-million-gen-zers-about-to-enter-us-workforce-and-change-it.html, Accessed on 3 March 2022.

- *Everything* is content and *all content* communicates. For Gen Zs, sharing a headline is a message. A photo is a 'vibe'. A video is a 'mood'. For a cutting-edge leader—to not bore his/her teams to death, these nonverbal but colourful mediums are required to get across what's felt.
- **Keep your texts and e-mails as short as possible.** Millennials have a 12-second attention span, whereas Gen Z has an average of eight seconds. Before going into the less crucial aspects, spell out the essential information. Mixing up the formatting in written communications with bulleted lists or bold text can also help Gen Z employees swiftly review messages for information that is relevant to them.
- **Cut the jargon out.** Gen Zers expect you to communicate in a personal and relatable way that speaks directly to them. To get across as a leader, you'll have to talk to them in *their* new-age lingo.
- **Keep it casual.** Work-talk doesn't have to be so buttoned-up. We can get to the point more quickly and have a little fun doing it. That means creating a shared joke with co-workers or capturing the ridiculousness of the moment with a clever emoji or goofy meme—and that's priceless. Sending 'That's fire' (meaning, that's amazing), 'KWIM' ('Know what I mean?') or an imp emoji (indicating rage, evil, or satanic activity) to a co-worker (or even their boss or client) is more likely to catch their attention than crafting a carefully-written email.
- **Keep your messages crisp and entertaining.** After all of this pandemic fatigue, these youngsters need some cheering up.
- **Make small talk.** Whether in the elevator, while going back home after work or during lunch breaks, find some time to initiate small talks. Ask your young employees about how their weekend went or what they plan on doing for

Christmas this year. They will find it charming.

- **Talk about social issues, talk about the impact your company is making on perhaps…the environment, world poverty or on gender equality.** Gen Z is the group that will change the world. They are aware of all issues that societies are facing. They want, and are continually working toward, ongoing and impactful change. Make them believe you are working towards changing the world, too. That appeals to them the most—*provided* its true. This generation smells dishonesty from multiple screens away; don't underestimate them because of their youth.

Five Takeaways for You To Skim Through:

- If millennials are the present of the business world, Gen Zs are the future. Make way, millennials.
- Most of us confuse millennials and Gen Zs, but in reality, both of these generations' priorities are very different.
- Gen Z wants financial stability, job security, a high-tech workplace and a digitally sound leader. They're also individual workers.
- Gen Z is progressive—tell them how your business is changing the world for the better and they'll be drawn to you like bees drawn to honey.
- Gen Zs may be young, but they're absolute powerhouses due to being digital natives, multi-taskers, great communicators, creative and business-minded.

7

DIVERSITY IN UNITY

Globalization for a start-up is exciting; you have to learn
so fast about the different cultures of the world.

—Adam Neumann, businessman and co-founder of WeWork

Has this happened to you? You strike up a conversation with a complete stranger, only to discover that you share surprising connections? I got a taste of this global interconnectedness back in a work conference in London.

I was sharing a table with two strangers—one from Tunisia and the other from Texas. It just so happened that the sitcom *The Big Bang Theory* came up in a conversation. As it happened, the science adviser for the show is an old pal of mine—and I never miss an opportunity to mention this. After all, I'm proud of his work!

To my amazement, I wasn't the only one who was connected to the show. The Tunisian researcher was related to one of the show's main characters, while the Texas researcher worked with a graduate school roommate of one of my friends. What a small world, right? Looking back, I don't know why we were so surprised. The world is getting smaller in ways we couldn't have imagined even 10 years ago. Tim Cook has said, 'The world is intertwined today, much more than it was when I was coming out of school. Because of that, you really need to have a deep understanding of cultures around the world. I have learned to not just appreciate this but celebrate it. The thing that makes the world interesting is our differences, not our similarities'[25] and I *totally* relate.

I have been spending a lot of my days in New Jersey and New York City since a couple of months. As I've walked around, I've heard some languages that I speak, some that I recognized and some that were totally foreign to me. As I considered this more, I concluded that the world is shrinking. I can easily travel to New Delhi or Jakarta, or meet residents who have visited my hometown, thanks to developments in communications, transportation and technology. You can communicate with folks all around the world either in person or over the internet. What are the main forces gluing the globe together?

Communication

We have come a long way in terms of communications in the past 150 years. It's easy for us to think all our generations were born with smartphones in their hands, facetiming their families and lovers; however, that was far from the case. The first ever telegraph message was sent by Samuel Morse in 1844 between Baltimore and Washington D.C. Never before could a message go from point to point without having to be carried by a runner, horse or boat.

---

[25]Corey Williams, 'Tim Cook discusses diversity, inclusion with students', *The Auburn Plainsman*, 6 April 2017, https://www.theplainsman.com/article/2017/04/tim-cook-discusses-diversity-inclusion-with-students, Accessed on 3 March 2022.

Fast-forward a few centuries, and wired telephone communications turned wireless and transformed into the smart-phones that we all cannot live without today.

Technology

Our world has also become smaller as a result of technological advancements. It has dramatically transformed how we communicate with one another and manage our work. Work groups were originally formed to design, manufacture and distribute physical commodities due to necessity. People in the group may see each other, communicate with one another and collaborate on projects. Many knowledgeable workers nowadays are miles, if not continents, apart from their teams. We may now take advantage of the sun's movement by shifting our operations throughout the world. In essence, a team may work on a concept or a product twenty-four hours a day with the correct coordination. Even with fast increase in transportation, we are no longer confined by those frameworks. We can create a team of people from far-flung places of the globe and generate incredible new ideas and products. I think that this is the promise that was launched by Morse, Marconi, Bell, Fulton and other pioneers.

Transportation

Transportation has also developed rapidly to allow us the freedom to move easily about the world. The discovery of the steam engine revolutionized land and maritime travel, allowing people to travel long distances on steam ships and railways. This paved the way for similar inventions in personal transportation—such as the internal combustion engine—which made automobile travel possible. With the invention of air travel, the world became even smaller, and it has only gotten faster over the last 100 years. We can travel to the next town or throughout the world with very little effort thanks to our contemporary infrastructure.

Social Media

I just had to dedicate a paragraph to this big guy. Social media might be the new-age God in terms of its impact on today's ideas, people, marketing, businesses and workplace cultures. It has definitely made our world shrink. It has, in fact, managed to convert the entire world into a global town.

'Software is eating up the world.' These are the words of one of the most successful venture capitalists of our time, Marc Andreessen. Everywhere you look, software, and social media in general, is taking over. You post a tweet and someone from across the planet retweets it or favourites it. Someone across the world writes a post on Facebook and it lands on your feed through shares. The Internet does provide tremendous reach. Now more than ever, getting information across the planet is as easy as a retweet, a like, a share, a repost, etc.

Today, *anyone* seeking to build a presence online only needs to target a few social media influencers and their message can reach millions. This ease of connectedness is what makes the world feel really small. The fact that you can like a status update by Barack Obama, or comment on the personal Twitter handle of Lady Gaga is monumental. Years ago, you would only hear what they had to say days later or after a lot of research; now, their voice is a click away.

Incorporating Globalization Within the Corporate Sphere

The world is going through globalization of culture and values. A Shanghai teenager will understand another teenager from New York, Rio or Seoul far better than his own grandfather! Language barriers are no longer a severe communication hurdle. Traveling abroad or communicating with people who spoke a different language were not commonplace a few decades ago. Today though, countries and communities around the world are becoming more connected. Travel is more affordable and accessible and businesses are operating on a global scale—irrespective of how large they are.

Another country is only a few hours away on a plane or a few time zones away via e-mail or Skype, which means more opportunities to meet new people, start new careers and travel to new places are becoming available—especially with the help of translation.

The world gets tinier and tinier, but are you, as a leader and a team-player, looking farther? Today's people are more connected than ever, but does this mean that cultural diversity have completely disappeared? It doesn't, yet it has resulted in the emergence of new huge cultural communities. The same TV series is watched by young people all across the world (Squid Games), and they all play the same video games and make the same memes.

As you learn more about cultural differences in the business jungle, you will encounter several more concepts. Spending time together at the dinner table (drinking and eating), for example, is one method to developing solid relationships when doing business in China. This is done in order to establish a stable network based on trust. This form of relationship is referred to as 'guanxi' in Chinese. In the United States, however, people don't often socialize with potential business partners unless necessary, to avoid embarrassing situations—drunken rambling, loud chewing, getting a little too personal—it's all a nightmare to Americans.

Another cultural difference would be the comfort of silence. In some countries, a few seconds of silence make the conversation uncomfortable. This happens in countries where the comfort of silence is low, such as in France, Italy and the United States. In Asian countries like Korea, Indonesia and Japan, however, the comfort of silence is high, which often results in Asians not speaking often during business meetings with people from Western countries. Asians are not likely to feel awkward if the conversation stops for as long as 30 seconds.

Clients and employees may find gestures that are customary in your own country insulting or strange, such as kissing somebody on the cheek, making eye contact and shaking hands strongly. Lean in to kiss a Japanese female client on the cheek as you greet them, and you're a pervert; give a tight hug to a South Korean teammate on a project's success, and you're unprofessional—so tread carefully.

Even punctuality is relative. When you deal with business partners, clients or colleagues from the United States, South Korea, Japan and Russia, you are expected to be on time, every time. I remember my Japanese clients glaring at me with a poker face as I'd entered the meeting 5 minutes late because the line to get a latte was extra-long that day. In Germany, you are even expected to be at least 10 minutes early for your appointment.

In Malaysia, however, expect to wait up to *an hour* if your counterpart stated that they would be about five minutes late. They are not required to explain either. In China, it is acceptable to be at least 10 minutes late, while in Mexico, it is pretty normal for people to be late by 30 minutes for a business meeting. In Morocco, personal meetings could be delayed by an hour and, in some cases, a day. When scheduling meetings in India, understand that being punctual is not one of their ways. It's kind of exhausting, isn't it? Not so much, once you develop a global mindset.

In the working world, an American leader may be flabbergasted that an Asian employee did not negotiate. However, he may not realize that speaking up assertively and asking for more money is considered disobedient and disrespectful to authority in Asian culture. An easy-going Australian sales director, who likes to joke around and tell long stories, may be taken aback by how blunt and all about business their German clients are.

Why am I telling you all this, you might ask? Because the new-age cutting-edge leader is well-aware of cultural differences and inclusive of all kinds of persons they have to work with. Although it can be a whirlwind in the beginning, as you learn to recognize different identities and cultures, you learn to build a super-team of powerhouses from across the world! .

A culturally knowledgeable leader understands that people from different parts of the world and even parts of the country have unique abilities and traits. A leader who embraces those differences and brings out the best in people, regardless of their cultural backgrounds, becomes the true ruler of the twenty-first century cutting-edge world.

When Cynt Marshall became CEO of NBA's Dallas Mavericks, she made a commitment to meet every member of the organization in the first 90 days. The first question she asked was: 'Tell me your life story.' The message Marshall wanted to send was that *the whole person matters*. Bring your own background, ideals and personality to the workplace. Don't put on your corporate mask. Don't act as if you're a superhero. The complete, authentic individual strengthens the company. These interviews helped to convey the concept that everyone matters, that everyone belongs, and that everyone contributes something unique to the team. They did, however, have another impact. 'I just fell in love with the people,' she reports. And for her, that is the most important duty of a new-age leader. 'There are only a few things that I need to do as a leader. I need to listen to the people… I need to learn from them because they are the experts. They're in touch with what's happening out there.'[26] The world is changing. And in turn, what organizations need from leaders is changing.

We know that when we surround ourselves with people who have a wide range of experiences and abilities, new ideas will emerge in a variety of ways to face the next obstacle. Diverse teams can help us identify blind spots and develop entirely new solutions. These advantages, however, do not occur by themselves. They emerge when managers and leaders draw out the diverse viewpoints and contributions of their teams and effectively capitalize on diversity. Basically, the new-age leader acts as the glue between various personalities and cultures to create sweet synergy. Take a look at these empires who did diversity right and profited off of it:

---

[26]Evan Sinar Maggie Wooll, 'What makes an inclusive leader? These 6 behaviors are a good start', BetterUp, 18 February 2021, https://www.betterup.com/blog/what-makes-an-inclusive-leader-and-6-ways-to-up-your-game, Accessed on 3 March 2022.

Alibaba Group	As the world's biggest e-commerce company, Alibaba Group serves hundreds of millions of users and hosts millions of merchants. Transactions on its online sites totalled $248 billion in 2017, more than those of eBay and Amazon.com combined. The secret to their success? Women. Chairman Jack Ma characterizes women as the 'secret sauce' driving Alibaba's supremacy in the online commerce business, taking the objective of gender equality to a new level. Women made up more than one-third of Alibaba Group's founders, and a similar ratio of top executives. 'Women's perseverance and attention to detail will outshine men in the age of robotics and machine learning.' Ma claimed.
Hilton	Hilton consistently shows up as a top diversity company. As one employee said, 'They love you for who you are and want to see you succeed. You have managers from the hotel and corporate that have your back and will push you to your fullest potential. Not many companies do that for you.' Hilton offers a very clear approach to diversity and inclusion for their workers.

Fenty Beauty	Popstar-turned-businesswoman Rihanna didn't come to play when she beat both Victoria's Secret and Kylie Cosmetics through her new brand. According to *Forbes*, she is now worth $1.7 billion, making her the world's wealthiest female musician.
	'Black women (and women of colour) wanted to support a Black brand that was made "by them, for them," while people across the board were happy to support a brand that had a finger on the pulse when it came to inclusivity,' comments marketing consultant Karina Scott, adding: 'Fenty Beauty spoke to all of us in the world that were treated like afterthoughts within the beauty industry... Now, if your brand isn't going to be inclusive then you'll become excluded!'[*]
	To make their products more inclusive, Fenty naturally created a team that was diverse, such that they could all understand what young women truly wanted from the complicated world of beauty products and lingerie.

[*]Eleanor Lees, 'What Is the Secret to Rihanna's Fenty Beauty Success and What Are the Top-Selling Products?', Newsweek, 6 August 2021, https://www.newsweek.com/rihanna-fenty-beauty-success-billionaire-best-products-1617018, Accessed on 3 March 2022.

L'Oréal	As *Forbes'* 'Top Multinational Performer', beauty company L'Oréal has a presence in 130 countries on five continents. To say that respect for multicultural diversity is at the core of this company's success would be a drastic understatement.
	To name a few of its many global projects, L'Oréal funds disability awareness workshops in India, matches staff with multicultural students in the Netherlands, and provides training to young adults in vulnerable Pakistani areas. The company also tops the list for gender equality. Women at L'Oréal account for 69 per cent of the workforce and 53 per cent of key positions.
	When it comes to multiculturalism in the workplace, L'Oréal offers a bevy of best practices to learn from.
Accenture	Global consulting and professional services firm Accenture has partnered with more than three-quarters of the Fortune Global 500 companies and serves clients in over 120 countries and across some 40 industries. At the core of these achievements is diversity in the workplace.

Accenture has a long history of valuing diversity as a source of creativity, innovation and competitive advantage. Leadership is holding the company accountable in a very public way as one of the first digital companies to reveal its staff demographics and progress toward internal diversity targets. Is this a risky strategy? Perhaps. Does it work? *Absolutely!*

According to Accenture's latest available data, the company is well on its way to achieving a dynamic workforce that's highly inclusive of various racial and ethnic backgrounds as well as veterans, military spouses and persons with disabilities. If you're looking for inspiration, Accenture is definitely a company to keep your eyes on.

Why Do You Really Need a Diverse Team?

• **Creativity.** When a group of people with similar interests gather around, they will come up with similar ideas. This is due to the fact that their thought processes are highly similar. If you shake things up by bringing in a broad group of people, you'll end up with a staff that's more prone to creativity and invention—two crucial factors for success. A diverse staff will be able to share different points of view and generate new ideas. A good example here is the Disney brand, which boasts a highly diversified enterprise with more than 2,00,000 employees worldwide.

Let's imagine a small organization with 10 to 15

people, all from the same gender group, culture, colour and ethnicity. Wouldn't their ideas and efficiency be limited or alike? They would look at a problem with the same lens, thereby resulting in a unidimensional outcome. And now, imagine the same organization with diverse employees. Their collective efficiency would go ten folds in that situation. Do I need to say more? You decide.

- **It's raining talent.** If you only pick from one section of society, you're automatically limiting your access to some super-talented candidates. By opting for diversity, you're opening the business up to a much wider talent pool and a much better chance of getting the right person through the door for a role.

- **Problems are solved, smooth like butter.** Diversity and inclusiveness aren't just nice-to-haves, they're business imperatives. The more diverse thoughts you can bring into a team, the greater the ideas.

   In other words, if you're searching for a competitive advantage, nothing beats approaching problems from diverse perspectives. And, owing to workplace diversity, you can approach problems from multiple perspectives at the same time.

   'If you can't fly then run, if you can't run then walk, if you can't walk then crawl, but whatever you do you have to keep moving forward,' stated Dr Martin Luther King Jr. But what if one person can't accomplish it all at once? That's when having a diverse group of people comes in handy.

   The team's 'flyers' see it from above, the 'walkers' from a levelled vantage point, and the 'crawlers' from below. This creates an ability to bring about resolutions that are fresh, new and innovative.

- **Higher productivity.** I know—I'm probably piling on

classic workplace jargon, but it's true: workplace diversity not only breeds creativity but also productivity. That's because diversity breeds creativity: the more diverse your workforce, the more diverse your brainstorming, the more unique your solutions and consequently, the more diversely productive your company will be. According to a McKinsey study, public corporations in the United States with diverse executive boards have a 95 per cent higher return on equity than those with homogeneous boards.

- **Your employees remain happy, simple.** Employees are more likely to feel comfortable and happy in an environment where inclusivity is a priority and when they're happy, they work better.

  The higher the team morale, the more productive employees are. Employees are more likely to be confident in their own unique abilities if they feel that diversity is encouraged and celebrated.

  Individual team members may be better able to share their ideas, become closer to their colleagues, and enjoy and take pride in their job if diversity is encouraged.

- **Understanding a wider range of clients and customers.** Renee James suggests that, 'There is a huge business case for diversity. You will be making products for people you don't understand, you don't interact with. If you don't have an inclusive, diverse workforce, it makes you myopic.'[27]

  Having a more diverse team will help your company gain

[27]TV Mahalingam, 'The global IT industry needs more women, says Intel's President Renée James', *The Economic Times*, 13 February 2015, https://economictimes.indiatimes.com/the-global-it-industry-needs-more-women-says-intels-president-rene-james/articleshow/46209587.cms?from=mdr, Accessed on 3 March 2022.

a broader understanding of your customers, what they want and what they look for. Your South Korean teammate can better handle a Japanese client as compared to your Indian peer; your Chinese teammate knows better what the kids in China want to buy today, as compared to your English-speaking powerhouse colleague, who helps you customize products for All-American customers instead.

You could be missing out on a huge group of potential customers that could be explored by not creating a diverse team.

- **An incredible image.** When any business promotes diversity, it is perceived as more relatable, socially responsible and human by a greater number of people—especially our precious millennials and Gen Zers. This can improve your overall brand reputation. You not only hire better young talent, but also sell more to more and more young shoppers. Not only that, according to an Indeed survey, one-fifth of job seekers believe that inclusivity and diversity in the recruiting process is one of the most important components in developing a positive connection or camaraderie with a firm during the interview stage.

Think about it, why did Victoria's Secret's sales tank even though they were untouchable in the early 2000s and 2010s? Well, young women belonging to the millennial and Gen Z eras wanted to see more women of different shapes and colours walking the ramp rather than only skinny, blonde, blue-eyed beauties; and the cutting-edge businesswomen Rihanna, founder of Fenty Beauty, recognized that. There has been a significant shift in how people, particularly young women, view beauty. We live in the #MeToo era. People demand diversity and representation, not only in terms of ethnicity and race, but also in terms of shape and body type. It can be a fatal shortcoming for shops to refuse to adapt or evolve.

Understanding the power of diversity now? It can make you or break you (of course, the latter happens only if you're *not* a cutting-edge inclusive leader.)

Understand the Challenges That Come With a Diverse Team (if It Doesn't Have an Inclusive New-Age Leader)

1) **Plaguing Prejudices:** Unfortunately, there are individuals who cannot tolerate people who are different from them. This can result in acts of racism, sexual harassment or even religious discrimination.

   Unfortunately, we all know that prejudice, stereotypes and bias are often ingrained in us and overcoming them takes humility and an openness to change. It's no wonder these issues are so sticky. Much of the time, it goes unnoticed or worse, unchecked by others. These behaviours very quickly damage an organization's culture and create toxicity.

2) **Different Preferences:** Communication issues can be somewhat common on diverse teams and for a wide variety of reasons. There may be language barriers, different communication styles or preferences, or people with hearing loss on your team. It's important to address these challenges before they become problematic.

   Let's say, for instance, your younger team members prefer to communicate via Slack or Facetime, while your older team members prefer to use e-mails or the plain old telephone. You may also find that someone who speaks English as a second language, or someone with hearing loss is struggling to follow the conversation in meetings. This leads to them feeling excluded and we all know that's *not* a pretty feeling.

3) **Cultural Clashes:** Sometimes, cultures can be so different that two people are unable to work together at all. Because of the emphasis on diverse teams, someone growing up in an ultra-conservative household in the southern United States may struggle to adapt to an ultra-liberal household in the Pacific Northwest and vice versa. This can result in low morale and productivity.

Misunderstandings can also be common when you bring people from different cultures together. For example, giving a thumbs up, using your left hand, or patting someone on the back are offensive in some cultures.

4) **Cracks in Communication:** When different teams collaborate and the default language is expected to be English, it can side-line peers who don't speak it as their first language.

Consider this: Arun, who just joined a large global company is excited and nervous. He speaks English, but it isn't his first language given that he's from India. Although his reading and writing skills in English are strong, he is still practicing verbal communication. During his first few meetings, he finds it hard to understand different accents and finds it challenging to understand English slang used by his American co-workers. He wishes they could slow down a bit and speak more clearly for him. Arun feels pressured to contribute early on and make a good first impression, but he's worried he might mess up and make a joke out of himself in front of his American colleagues.

This shows an organization's failure to build an inclusive workplace. Arun is clearly being left out of the conversation and those leading the meeting aren't making any effort to recognize that he's a little out of the loop.

5) *Too Many* **Opinions:** Diverse teams may also open up the door for more debates and arguments which can lead to fewer

decisions being made. Different peers approach the same problem and present their thoughts in different ways due to their diverse backgrounds and experiences. Employees who do so are incredibly useful to your company because they will continue to drive new ideas and discover problems. However, having too many points of view can make it difficult to find a common ground. In a sea of ideas, particularly unique solutions to issues may go ignored. Too many viewpoints can jeopardize a team's ability to meet deadlines and act.

6) **Teammates Feeling Excluded (and Naturally, Bitter):** When people don't feel included, the cost is deeply personal. It also hurts the team. They don't show themselves. They may withhold opposing or counterintuitive ideas and refuse to engage in brainstorming sessions for fear of further alienating themselves from the group. They are concerned that their opinions and comments will not be treated with the same openness and seriousness as those of others. They don't bring up their distinct personality, history, or interests in discussion. They do not take significant risks or accomplish significant achievements. They aren't observed. They have self-censorship. What does it cost the team? Employees who feel excluded are 25 per cent less productive on subsequent assignments, have a 50 per cent higher chance of leaving and are less motivated to put in extra effort for the team.

Five Takeaways for You To Skim Through:

• The world is shrinking—not literally but because language, culture and media are being shared in seconds across continents. Today, Shanghai, Mumbai and Washington, D.C. are more connected than you realize.

• Nonetheless, the cutting-edge leader realizes that despite globalization, cultures and identities are different—especially in the world of business. There is diversity in this global unity.

- Diverse teams in the workplace are the present and the future. They lead to more innovation, synergy, problem-solving and catering to wider audiences.
- Diverse teams also face challenges—like cultural clashes, communication errors, racism and slow decision-making due to too many opinions.
- The cutting-edge leader is needed because of these very challenges. The cutting-edge leader handles these issues smooth like butter.

8

BREAKING BAD BARRIERS

*Inclusivity means not 'just we're allowed to
be there,' but we are valued. I've always said: smart
teams will do amazing things, but truly diverse
teams will do impossible things.*

—Claudia Brind-Woody, Vice President & Managing Director
for Global Intellectual Property Licensing at IBM

Years ago, I received an urgent call from a client, a CEO of a tech company, talking about my peer Chi-Ling from Taiwan. 'Though Chi-Ling is technically doing a good job, her accent is driving me *nuts* and I have a hard time understanding her. Please replace her immediately with someone else,' she half-yelled.

My team could have easily replaced Chi-Ling with somebody else to fix the issue immediately, but replacing her with someone else would cost the company more time and money to train someone new. I encouraged my client to give Chi-Ling one more chance. During a series of one-on-one meetings, I coached Chi-Ling to speak clearly and slowly. I also coached our client to be culturally sensitive and aware about the communication differences. After a few weeks, both my client and Chi-Ling were happily working together. In fact, Chi-Ling turned out to be a long-term employee: someone who became a key contributing team member of the tech company.

The cutting-edge leader brings together superpowers across the globe to break barriers and create absolute magic. As Adam Neumann has rightly said, 'How do you change the world? Bring people together. Where is the easiest big place to bring people together? In the work environment!'[28]

How Do You Break Bad Barriers Like a Boss?

1) **You Understand Differences:** You cannot tackle differences if you don't acknowledge them. The cutting-edge leader is always aware of any internal, unconscious bias that they may hold and understands that everyone does carry some level of this bias with them. You can admit it: nobody's perfect.

   If a team leader admits these shortcomings in himself or herself, he or she can then take steps to correct them. Take these steps to ensure that you are acting fairly and respectfully in your day-to-day. 'You can't change what you don't watch. Without effort, we are all susceptible to unconscious bias. Everyone has their own biases, but being aware of your company's female team member statistics and being actively interested in bettering them is a first step.'[29]

---

[28]David Gelles, 'The WeWork Manifesto: First, Office Space. Next, the World.', *The New York Times,* 17 February 2018, https://www.nytimes.com/2018/02/17/business/the-wework-manifesto-first-office-space-next-the-world.html, Accessed on 3 March 2022.

[29]Jocelyn Mangan, 'Diversity At Work Is Essential, And It's Everyone's Responsibility', *Forbes,* 5 October 2017, https://www.forbes.com/sites/forbeshumanresourcescouncil/2017/10/05/diversity-at-work-is-essential-and-

states, Jocelyn Mangan, chief operating officer at Snagajob, and I cannot help but agree.

- Make sure that you are listening to and valuing all contributions equally.
- Speak up to challenge inappropriate behaviour of all levels, from outright discrimination to micro-aggressions. You're then a true hero to your team.
- Do not police culture. Allow people to be authentic. (For example, a co-worker should feel safe discussing the trip they took over the weekend with their partner, regardless of gender or race.)
- Remove biases in processes to make sure that decision-making is fair and even. For instance, a co-worker shouldn't be patronized just because they're Asian or that they're a woman.

---

2) **Don't Act 'Woke' Just for The Sake of It:** A tiny Gen Z lingo lesson: the term 'woke' in today's internet lingo means being aware or well-informed in a political or cultural sense. It describes someone who has 'woken up' to issues of social injustice and is inclusive.

Now, most leaders merely act 'woke' just for brownie points; don't be like them. You may attract talent initially, but they won't stick around. People, especially young workers, sense ingenuity a mile away. So, walk the walk. Trueness is the secret sauce in creating a better employee experience for diverse teammates.

3) **Hang Out With Those Different From You:** Just reading about a different age group or different culture won't honestly do much. As a forward-thinking leader, you must

---

its-everyones-responsibility/?sh=53cea2b01537, Accessed on 3 March 2022.

surround yourself with people who are unlike you. When you're looking for new insights, ask your coworkers who they believe might be able to help. A diverse team is more productive and achieves better results.

4) **Do You Know What It's Like Being Them?** What if the roles were completely reversed and you were in the other person's shoes—living in a new country and working with foreigners? Now, throw being thousands of miles away from family, friends and your comfort zone into the mix. This is exactly how many of your foreign co-workers feel when they live in *your* country.

By being culturally sensitive to the fact that your foreign co-workers moved far away from their homes to work in your country and for your company, it may help you become more understanding and patient in dealing with them. Try to be aware of the challenges they had to—and continue to—face on a daily basis.

5) **The 'Small Issues' Aren't So Small After All:** When you witness someone being rude or dismissive to someone else, be brave and call it out. Don't focus on finding fault but stating what you notice and suggesting alternatives that include everyone.

It sounds something like this: 'You know, not everyone in our group celebrates Christmas. I'm wondering what we could do this holiday season to allow those who celebrate the holiday to do so while also allowing others, regardless of religion, to participate.'

Perhaps you've noticed that an employee is actively or unconsciously neglecting the contributions of female team members in meetings. Get back to and amplify their points with a comment like, 'I agree with what Jane and Sarah said earlier about…'

6) **Building Bonds With Everyone, *Equally*:** Inclusive leadership cannot be transactional. Inclusive leaders spend time getting to know their team members, peers and other employees, learning what matters to them and what they require to be successful. They understand that each individual is a complete person with more to give than just numbers. Understanding peers as equal human beings goes beyond tolerance and accommodation when it comes to building connections.

People feel respected, valued and appreciated when true relationships are built. Everyone can feel more comfortable extending themselves, taking risks, giving honest feedback and contributing their various experiences and viewpoints to the job in an environment of respect and admiration.

7) **Being Careful of Everyone's Different Needs:** My friend Sally recalled an experience where her co-worker Lexie, needed extra shifts during the holidays to afford medical care for an ill family member back in Hong Kong. Their team leader Markus brought the team together and asked if everyone would be willing to donate one of their shifts to help Lexie. Sally described this experience as being inclusive because the leader Markus, was sensitive to the unique needs of one of their team members and felt that if they needed help, the leader and team would do this for them. He understood Lexie's helplessness and stress of being miles away from family when they needed her. And that instantly made his entire team fall in love with him as a leader.

8) **An Open Mind:** 'Their culture is pretty weird!' Grace titters as she watches her Japanese co-workers bow to one another after work's over. 'That's not how you say goodbye in *my* country!'

Have you ever heard those words, or have those thoughts crossed your mind? Yes, unfortunately, you have. Now tell me, how many times did you intervene and tell your co-workers they were being ignorant? Many teams have such people who think the world revolves around their culture and prefer to stay in the comfort zone working with people similar to themselves, and cutting-edge leaders know well-enough how to call them out: *gently, of course.* And for that, the new-age leader needs to have an open mind themselves.

It's important to remember that leadership is not only about opening doors and growing others. It's also about *keeping an open mind* while opening doors and growing others. Vivian Maza states that, 'Although no one individual is responsible for creating an inclusive culture (remember, it takes commitment from everyone), your leadership team ultimately sets the tone for the entire company. If you are in a leadership position and want to see change in your organization, first reflect on your own behavior and biases. Are you publicly praising all deserving employees for their outstanding work and providing recognition as often as it's earned?'[30] Building a culture of inclusion isn't like turning on a light switch. It takes deliberate actions, starting with *you* being respectful of everyone.

9) **Use Your Power To Challenge Privilege:** Be open to learning. Ask questions respectfully. Do your own research by listening to voices from different cultures and walks of life outside of the workplace. Be ready to alter workplace norms if deemed necessary. If you approach this knowing that you have work

---

[30]Vivian Maza, 'Building A Workplace Culture That Supports Employees—Especially Women', *Forbes*, 6 December 2017, https://www.forbes.com/sites/forbeshumanresourcescouncil/2017/12/06/building-a-workplace-culture-that-supports-employees-especially-women/?sh=4414c17b1412, Accessed on 3 March 2022.

to do, you're already on the right path. If a team member has a new strategy or idea, encourage them to try it out. Give them the autonomy they need to get the results you both want.

Take turns giving your team members high-level projects to work on. See that work is divided evenly and everyone has an opportunity to reach their potential. When they do succeed, make sure you shine a light on those successes and celebrate them. Question yourself and the common practices around you. Seek feedback from the voices you're trying to amplify. Asking, 'How can I be a better leader, a better friend and a better ally?' is a great step. However, don't rely on them to be your teachers. You'll have to do much of this work on your own.

Inclusive leaders use both their privilege and high standing in the company to make way for positive change. This includes actions as well as words.

- Use your voice to actively challenge bad behaviour and unfair practices. Start those hard conversations at a higher level.
- Do not speak ill of anyone or their culture behind their back. If there is an issue that needs to be addressed, do so head-on and approach the issue directly.
- Do not get personal with an employee—just because they messed up professionally doesn't mean you attack their race, country or religion.
- Admit when you make a mistake and learn from it. Showing humanity and owning up to your missteps makes you an attractive, genuine leader.
- Stand by your word and speak the truth. If you are transparent with your team, they will trust you. This creates a stronger team all-around.

10) Choose What You Say *Carefully:* Communication amongst team members can be difficult when you have a varied workforce. Many members of your staff may not speak English as a first language. Language limitations may cause team members to communicate ineffectively and have difficulty understanding one another. Failure to completely comprehend instructions may result in a considerable reduction in productivity and team cohesion.

For example, female employees may talk more politely, avoid swear words and use more tag questions than male employees, which could lead to misunderstandings. Younger employees may use a different language and slangs which older generations are unfamiliar with (read the previous chapters for more insight).

Hiring multilingual employees to undertake translations can help you avoid these problems. You can also choose from a variety of translation apps on the market. You could even send your personnel to language schools to study new languages. This will also help them communicate with overseas consumers and clients as a side benefit.

- Agree on a common language and an appropriate workplace discourse to avoid miscommunication.
- Although this can be difficult, try to hire as many bilingual employees as possible. It's also a significant competitive advantage having employees with advanced bilingual abilities, especially if you're an international organization.
- Be patient with employees; understandably, it might take them a little while to adjust. Even if their English is basic, they will soon learn if given the chance. Offer support and tell your employees to do the same.

- Encourage your employees to ask for clarification if they are unsure about what they're being asked to do. Better to clarify matters at the outset then rectify faults later.

11) **Create Unwritten Rules:** Vladimir was a brilliant engineer whose promotion to engineering manager included relocating to the US. His boss became concerned when he noticed Vladimir rarely spoke in meetings, even the meetings Vladimir was leading. He shared his observation with Vladimir and asked if everything was alright. Vladimir shared: 'Where I am from, it's a sign of disrespect to interrupt someone or cut them off when they are speaking. I want the people on my team to know I respect them, but I sometimes don't know how to make myself heard.'

At the US office, spirited talks with everyone talking and interrupting were the norm. Vladimir's boss suggested that he teach his staff that raising his hand or saying 'excuse me' meant he wanted to be heard on a particular subject. These tactics allowed him to be heard without having to change a long-held opinion or habit. This one example points out why it's so important to avoid making assumptions and to instead proactively look for ways to make sure all employees are comfortable.

What Are Some Things an Inclusive Team-Player/Co-Worker/ Leader Doesn't Say?

- When a white colleague says to a black colleague, 'You're so articulate' or 'You speak really well,' it implies that they expected the individual in question to be less articulate—and are astonished when they aren't.

- 'You're pretty smart for a woman' or 'You're pretty intelligent for a Black man.'
- 'What's your name, again? Soon-Shim? Or Soo-Kim? Or, is it Soo-Young?'
- If you have a foreign colleague, just *know how to say their name* instead of using the hit-and-trial method. It's that simple.
- 'My boss is a crazy chick. Women can be such emotional fools.'
- 'It's impossible to understand your accent...come again?' (Say: Pardon me, I couldn't quite catch that point. Could you repeat yourself, please?')
- 'Where are you from again...Japan, China or Vietnam?'
- 'Your name is so difficult to say. Can you tell me an easier way to call you? Perhaps an English name?'
- 'Is this your real hair?' to a Black person or 'Are these your real features? I heard every Asian person gets plastic surgery done!' (Just don't do it.)
- (Interrupting a woman) 'Well, actually, I think...' (Wait for the person to finish their thought. And if you like their idea, give them credit.)
- 'She's just a dumb blonde.'
- 'Well, get used to it. This is how we do it in my country/ this country.'
- 'You're gay? You should meet my gay friend!'
- 'You do so much despite being handicapped!' (Yikes.)
- To an older employee: 'Do you even know how to use Facebook?'
- 'Why do you wear that thing?' (Never ask someone why they wear something—whether that's a hijab or hair extensions. As long as they do their job well, it doesn't really matter, right?)

- 'You're so articulate for your age.'
- 'No offense, but....'
- 'You're pretty fun for an Asian person!'
- 'You're all dressed up today. Have a date with your dream man?' ('You look nice today.' That is, if you feel very comfortable in your office environment. Complimenting a female co-worker on appearance can be dicey at times. It's probably the best office etiquette to just leave it alone.)
- 'Maybe in your country, this idea works, but here...'
- 'Are you pregnant?'
- 'Being pregnant makes you act stupidly.'
- 'You're finally back from maternity leave. Are you going to stay?'
- 'Why do you still work after having kids?'
- 'You're lucky to have a job as a foreigner in this country.'
- 'Didn't you just visit your hometown a few months ago?'
- 'You're being overemotional...'
- Calling a woman co-worker 'hon', 'sugar', 'sweetheart', 'darling' or 'baby'.
- 'Come on! It was just a joke.' (A good team player and leader takes accountability and corrects themselves instead.)

Five Takeaways for You To Skim Through:

- The modern leader has to be global. And who's a global leader? A leader who is inclusive and treats all equally.
- The cutting-edge leader understands the needs and ways of working of *all* their teammates, and not just those who belong to his country, race or gender.
- The cutting-edge leader is sensitive towards foreign workers who have left their countries to work. He/She makes sure

they feel included even if they cannot speak English or understand everything in one go.

- The cutting-edge leader creates an entire culture of diversity and inclusivity. How will teammates work together if the leader himself/herself creates division?
- The cutting-edge leaders choose what to say, carefully. And of course, he/she knows what *not* to say to lose respect in the minds of his teammates.

9

FROM MACHINE TO ORGANISM: THE NEXT-GEN ORGANIZATION

When leaders throughout an organization take an active, genuine interest in the people they manage, when they invest real time to understand employees at a fundamental level, they create a climate for greater morale, loyalty, and, yes, growth.[31]

—Patrick Lencioni, American author of best-selling book *Five Dysfunctions of a Team*

In the twentieth century (sounds like a long time ago, doesn't it?) the workplace was a rigid place where employees conformed to cultural norms like wearing a shirt and tie and working 9 to 5. Employees used to spend most of their time in the office working under a manager's direction, and at the end of their one-year anniversary, receive a performance review. Nobody fancies that anymore!

What makes a company a great place to work *in today's times?* Is it the perks? The location? The brand name? Maybe the compensation? No. I say it's a company's modern, cutting-

---

[31]Patrick Lencioni, *The Five Dysfunctions of a Team*, Wiley India Pvt Ltd, 2006.

edge culture.

We bet you've heard of popular companies like Facebook, Adobe, Twitter, Google and Chevron. Are you able to figure out what they all have in common? Yes, it is correct. It's because of their fantastic work environment. They all have one thing in common: they can't seem to get enough of their company's culture. It is, in fact, rather stunning. These companies' personnel are not only polite and courteous to one another, but they also excel at loving what they do and executing it to the best of their abilities. The interests of these employees are the same interests as the company. As a result, their work culture and employee productivity propel on its own. No yelling managers, no feudal leaders, no workplace stress—only happiness and productivity. Sounds heavenly, right?

Today's modern workplace, is a fluid, casual environment, where work-life balance is championed and, depending on your company culture, some employees might even come to work dressed in sweatpants from time to time.

Modern corporate executives have discovered that traditional, restrictive working styles hinder efficiency and are unable to tackle new-age difficulties, such as staff cooperating efficiently over great distances. The modern workplace has a diverse workforce, is growing more responsive to issues and is becoming less dependent on physical locations. Employees increasingly use current collaborative software such as Skype and Google Docs to communicate more effectively with their global colleagues in real time as they desire, without being micromanaged. A perfect blend of modern culture and modern tools.

Unlike the tradition organization, the modern organization doesn't see a leader as a ruler of an empire. Neither is this new organization a money-making mass machine meant to only produce profits and results; this modern organization is an organism—a team of living beings, who need to remain motivated, happy and mentally stable.

Having a modern workplace culture is an effective way to attract and retain talent. Employees want to work for organizations that offer flexible scheduling, work-from-home arrangements and growth opportunities, and they're leaving jobs that burn them out, especially younger workers with several other job options. Modern workplace culture demonstrates—through more than just words—that employee growth and well-being is *top priority.*

Modern workplace culture is no longer a 'nice-to-have' for organizations. It is a *must-have* to attract and retain talent. Expectations will continue to evolve and those who haven't activated modern workplace culture will be left behind. A modern workplace culture should be a goal for every business and every cutting-edge leader. It is not the duty of a creative leader to have all of the ideas; rather, it is to foster a culture in which everyone can have ideas and feel respected.

It's a sign of a forward-thinking, open-minded organization that has engaged and motivated workers. This engagement filters through and has a positive knock-on effect with customers. Happy staff deliver better results to customers. You cannot have happy customers if you have grumpy, disgruntled staff, it's like oil and water—the two don't mix.

The goal of most workplaces is to only get things done which, in my opinion, is why exactly they don't get things done. Don't understand? Let me explain—when a company focuses on its workers' happiness and career growth rather than mercilessly demanding results, it ironically gets the best results from them.

When we have a healthy workplace culture, it sets the stage for doing good work. In my opinion, culture is the most significant factor that influences work relationships, employee happiness and productivity. We agree with the phrase attributed to Peter Drucker: 'Culture eats strategy for breakfast.' You can have the most incredible strategy imaginable, but if you don't have a healthy culture in which to execute your strategy, it's just mere words on a page.

In my opinion, *nothing* impacts employee engagement more than workplace culture, not money, not materialistic perks, not even healthy competition. The secret to improving employee engagement is culture. Think others won't be aware of your culture? Think again. Whether it be partners, consumers, stakeholders or board members, your culture will determine your interactions with them. Humans, from entrepreneurs and executives to regular managers, are the world's top innovators. How they collaborate, communicate and collaborate with others can either help or hinder their achievement. Is your company's or team's culture encouraging or inhibiting innovation?

You will be able to fill your job openings if your workplace is bound by regulations and laws, the work is uninteresting and the employees are not regarded and valued—but they will not stay. The best folks will be the first to leave. They'll get the distinct smell of a dreadful workplace in their nostrils and start looking for a new employment. They'll say, 'See you!' and then disappear a few weeks later. Let me tell you some other ways a feudal, old-school culture fails in the modern era of business:

- **Your workers/peers feel *zero* passion for what they do.** If you look around at your colleagues, does everyone's face seem like they just found out they need a root canal?

  Bad attitudes create a self-fulfilling prophecy. All of that negativity is a result of the culture, but it also feeds the overall dreary feeling in the office. Worse, it impedes everyone's capacity to complete tasks. When working with persons who have bad attitudes, 93 per cent of employees claim they are less productive.

- **Fatigue, fatigue and more fatigue.** Feel tired all the time? Run! You're stuck in a toxic workplace. The mental toll of working under such pressure leads to a lack of sleep and even insomnia. Excessive weariness can cause a person to lose their sex drive, retreat socially, have stomach problems and migraines, among other things. Burnout and job loss might result from feeling weary all of the time. It's pretty simple: you cannot do well at work if you're fatigued.

- **Ruined image and scope for gaining new talent.** Once it's on the internet, it's there forever; once a post about a company's toxic work culture goes viral, consider the company is as good as finished. Negative word of mouth will ruin your capacity to acquire the best employees, but anonymous review sites like Glassdoor can be devastating for businesses because they are held to a higher standard. Everyone suffers the repercussions of their actions. With so much research and data pointing to the need for a supportive workplace culture, this topic can no longer be ignored by the organizational leadership.

  Last year, comedian and TV host Ellen DeGeneres was at the centre of allegations that her show was a toxic workplace, a story that dominated news headlines and social media, with some fellow celebrities taking sides. Tesla has been in the news this year after a former employee won a multimillion-dollar lawsuit alleging racist harassment at the firm. But these are just two examples that make the news. From Amazon to Uber, several notable workplaces have come under scrutiny...even the biggest of business empires aren't safe.

- **No work-life balance.** Does your work interfere with your normal life? In other words, are you able to keep your personal life and your work life separate without difficulty? If not, it's probable that your workplace is contributing to your lack of work-life balance. This simply implies that your work will most likely follow you home from the workplace, whether or not you want it to. Work-life balance blurs the lines between job and home, and it often exacerbates work-related stress by preventing people from resting. This leads to employees hating their jobs, being more absent from work (literally and figuratively) and only putting the bare minimum during assigned tasks. And of course, there's *zero loyalty.*

- **Your precious human resources fall sick often.** Millennials may be dubbed the 'burnout generation,' but a toxic workplace has a detrimental impact on everyone. According to research, too stressful work settings promote absenteeism and cause people to become sick more frequently. The financial implications of employee absenteeism are obvious. According to the Centers for Disease Control and Prevention, decreased productivity from missed work costs companies $225.8 billion per year, or $1,685 per employee. What do you think? Employee health is directly influenced by the culture of your business. It shouldn't take an expert to tell you that healthy employees will be more productive.

- **Constant confusion leads to no deadlines being met.** Nobody is clear on their roles or responsibilities. Crossed wires are common, and people are always left out of the loop. Team members can barely tell which way is up and blame games are the norm…all too familiar? There, there.

Toxic workplaces are breeding grounds for drama and confusion. That's because these negative environments are often accompanied by a lack of trust, ineffective communication, and power struggles. Those issues make it all the more challenging for team members to collaborate, so projects, meetings and relationships frequently run off the rails.

What Is Happiness at Work?

- A positive and pleasant feeling at work.
- Excitement at the thought of going to work.
- Liking the people you interact with at work.
- Feeling safe and appreciated at the workplace.
- Being able to associate some meaning and value to your work.
- Having some fun through the process of working.
- Having a leader as an *ally* rather than a boss.

How Does the Cutting-Edge Leader Create a Captivating Culture for His Co-Workers?

1) **Be Picky:** We've already pointed out the fact that a happy work culture attracts good people. But every talent out there is not best for your work culture. That means you need to get a little picky about the people you add to your team. The greatest candidate on paper might be the worst person to bring into your office. Look for the intangibles. Be very aware of how you feel around the person. Do they appear to be more concerned with the positives than the negatives? Do they laugh? Do they appear to be smiling? Do they appear to build and foster relationships? While their performance history is crucial, a person who brings dread and gloom to the workplace will destroy productivity and motivation.

The hiring process is where the process of creating a good workplace begins. Employers must devote a significant amount of time while interviewing possible candidates for a position in their organization to examining the expressions, reactions and genuineness of the candidates. Give yourself a pat on the back if you've already done a wonderful job by hiring exceptional people for your team.

2) **And Be Kind:** Get in the habit of being grateful and showing gratitude for what you have. It can be a small thing: I am thankful for this cup of coffee, for the sun coming out today. As corny as it sounds, your cheerfulness will be contagious to your teammates and subordinates. Leaders never complain or sulk. Leaders give strength and courage. When communicating with your staff, keep the focus on the positive. Make a point of highlighting their successes and abilities. Remind them that they are a valuable asset to your firm and that they have a lot to contribute. This is a potent motivator that will help your employees develop a 'can-do' mentality.

My cousin's daughter told me her leadership team brought in ice cream and a whole shebang of fixings. They lined everything up on a table and dished out sundaes for their employees. The random aspect of this event really put people around the office in a good mood.

You don't necessarily have to bring in ice cream to boost morale in the workplace. But you can definitely do something kind for your employees—on the fly. It feels a lot more genuine than a generic speech on values and goodness. As is rightly said that leadership is more about opening the heart than it is about skill and tactics. Leadership is about inspiring others and oneself. Human experiences, not processes, are at the heart of great leadership. Leadership is a human action that originates from the heart and considers the hearts of others, not a formula or a programme. It's a mindset, not a routine.

3) **Form a Community**: Make a point of encouraging people to say hi to each other. It's quite simple: you have to begin greeting them yourself and they'll reciprocate. Sounds a little too generic, but it is actually an incredible way to build a sense of workplace community and something that busy and focused people forget. Start by making it a policy to have your executives and managers make sure to take the time to say hi. Choose ambassadors from all different levels and areas of your company to do the same. Acknowledging people can change the entire atmosphere and make your workplace be a much nicer place.

4) **Your Brand Is Your Purpose**: What does your brand stand for? What are the problems it addresses or solves? Does it serve the customer or help them in any possible way? Questions like these may sound very moralistic, but they're super important in making your workers feel like absolute superheroes. They work harder because they feel they're making a genuine difference.

Coca-Cola promises to refresh the mind, body and spirit; to inspire moments of optimism, create value and make a difference. This is what Coca-Cola stands for and that they strongly believe in spreading happiness. Coca-Cola also promotes an inclusive work culture that is rich in diverse people, talent and ideas.

5) **Let Your Workers Be a Little Selfish Every Now and Then**: Part of the secret to being happy at work is to encourage people to have personal career goals. When people feel that they are working toward something, the day-to-day politics and stresses of the workplace don't matter as much. Each

challenging day can be better tolerated because it is a means to a personal end. People are able to separate themselves from their jobs and not become mired in the negativity when they are focused on reaching personal goals.

6) **Break the Monotony**: Sitting at a desk all day long or working on tricky projects back-to-back can be overwhelming—as well as extremely boring. And if that's all your employees do at work every day, it'll eventually become mind-numbing. This is why it's critical that you surprise your co-workers and go above and beyond your normal job routine (occasionally). If you're stuck for ideas, try meeting your team outside of work at their favourite lunch spot or telling everyone to start their day on Monday doing the one thing that makes them happy. These are simple ideas that will make your team members super productive even if their day is super busy. Practice this and see yourself how rested and refreshed your employees feel at work, allowing them to tackle every task with utmost productivity.

7) **Pet Their Self-Esteem (Egos)**: Did you know that feeling unappreciated is the main reason why Americans quit their jobs? It's true. So, what can you do to ensure your team is being consistently recognized for their hard work? Create a system that makes it easy—it's not as complicated as it seems. It could be something like this: the entire team gathers around in a circle and everyone goes around the room calling out someone whose work we want to recognize. You can also create a monthly or quarterly award for the team member who most embodies your core values.

8) **Health Is Wealth, *For Real*:** Encourage everyone in your office to 'live a healthy life', as much as it makes you sound like a mother. While a health lecture may seem like a good way to assist individuals improve their health, it is unlikely to

pique your team's interest. To make wellness work, you must gain buy-in from your employees and make it pleasurable for them. Yoga, healthy potluck lunches, step/fitness challenges with Jawbone trackers, and delicious nutritious snacks have all proven to be a hit at some of the companies I've visited.

Introduce activities that will make it easier for employees to adopt and sustain healthy behaviours both inside and outside of work, whether it's through healthy eating habits, mindfulness techniques, or some easy physical exercises. Do you want to know how to develop a wellness culture? Here's what you might like:

- Create and share a list of healthy restaurants and dining near your office. Save your employees from wasting their time googling 'yummy food near me'—believe me, they do it more often than you realize.
- Offer corporate discounts for gyms and fitness clubs.
- Host a yoga day every week, hire a professional yoga instructor and let your team members calm their mind.

9) **Party Time:** It's a proven fact that having co-worker pals makes going to work more enjoyable. It contributes to the feeling that you and your co-workers are all 'in this together'. Having regular entertaining activities in the midst of work allows your staff to interact on a more personal level with their peers.

Offsites are one of my personal favourite ways to get people mingling, but you can also do things like a Happy Hour once a month or half-day Fridays in the summer to hang out together. The magic of a summer beach day with the team cannot be overstated.

10) **The Power of Power Naps:** If your employees are exhausted,

you can't expect them to be in a good mood. Create a location specifically created to allow your employees to rest if you have the space and some extra money in your budget. Companies like Google, Facebook and Proctor & Gamble are investing in nap pods for a reason: well-rested employees are happier than their grumpy, sleepy colleagues.

11) **Press the Pause Button:** Emotional Intelligence Guru, Daniel Goleman and a few others, have shown that even a few minutes of paying attention to our breathing or meditating helps us to declutter the mind and increase focus—a fundamental prerequisite for happiness. Let your employees go for a nice walk, get some warm chamomile tea or share some interesting stories with their peers. They don't have to work seven hours straight to get work done.

12) **Meet and Greet:** To reduce the likelihood that all of your employees are getting stressed out and morale is tanking, check in with your team on a regular basis—even once a week—to see how they're doing. Regularly solicit feedback from them to determine whether any changes need to be made. Don't let potential problems fester unnecessarily.

13) **If You're Taking Feedback, Learn To Give It Too:** Your team craves feedback, yet much of corporate communication seems perilously broken. In a recent survey, it was found that less than one-third of employees said their company would be willing to change practices based on employee feedback. When employees don't feel heard, they don't feel respected or happy in the workplace. When this happens, they begin to dream of greener pastures.

Improve your existing employee feedback program or implement one that actually listens to the ideas of your best people. Set up a quarterly or monthly meeting where the whole team can talk through smart suggestions, and be sure to recognize when the company has implemented an employee-suggested concept. This way, your team can see their contributions and that feedback really does matter.

14) **Get Them On-the-Go:** It's time to think about your company's employee wellness program. Healthy employees are happier, more likely to show up, and more likely to add positive value to your company. Companies from L.L. Bean to Johnson & Johnson have invested in wellness programs because they know employees who feel their best also put their best foot forward at work, not just on their morning jog.

Plus, the endorphins released during exercise can lead to an improved mood. Your wellness program could be as complicated as a large-scale, incentivized initiative or as simple as getting the team to take a yoga class or a long walk during lunch. Whatever you decide, make sure wellness and movement become important parts of your company's culture.

15) **Ditch the Favouritism, *Please:*** Your employees will notice if you give a handful of team members preferential treatment. There's an easy fix: do your best to treat everyone fairly. Don't direct 100 per cent of your compliments to one person—or even one team. Spread them around, and have the same rules and expectations for everyone.

16) **The Power of a Pooch:** Could a dog be your company's best friend? Research has found employees are more productive, happier and less stressed when they can bring their four-legged friends into the office. A 2010 study discovered that just the presence of a dog in the office led to employees collaborating more effectively. Pet lovers will be happier having a Tommy or Sally in the office, and taking pets for walks throughout the day can help keep your best people moving, combat stress and return to their work refreshed.

17) **Get Out of Your Private Room:** If you are in a leadership position, everyone already knows. You don't need an office to prove it. And, there are many benefits to working amongst your team, rather than cooping yourself up in a closed-off room. Your co-workers will be more willing to share their thoughts and ideas if they can just walk up to their managers' desk, and ask questions instead of queueing up outside their offices or checking with the receptionist to see them.

At Stripe, for example, CEO Patrick Collison doesn't have an office or even a desk for that matter. He changes where he works every day to make sure that he stays in touch with everyone in the company on a more casual level. This not only gives your employees a voice, it also enables teams to work better and faster together. When everyone knows what others are working on and feel like they can ask anyone anything, decisions can be made straight away.

18) **A Salary Hike Never Hurts Anyone:** If you want to make your workers happy, do something very simple: give them a salary hike. You don't have to boost it by double or something, but at least increase it by a certain amount so that they feel happy about it. The bottom line is that if they feel happy about it, they will certainly do better and that is exactly what we want in our workplace, don't we?

19) **And Neither Does a Vacation:** No, you don't have to spend too much money for this. Just plan a weekend getaway at a nearby resort and set a few goals for your people. Tell them that whoever does it better will have the opportunity to go away to a luxury resort for the weekend. If you do this once in every two months, people in your company will want to work harder, and in that way, you will balance the culture at work.

20) Lastly, Learn To Ditch Your Professionalism (Oftentimes): This one sounds a bit crazy, right? It's true, however.

It's time we start blurring the lines in who we are at home and who we are at work. I've talked to far too many people who say, 'You've never seen that side of me, because I don't act that way at work.' I even remember a time where I asked a colleague, how their weekend was and they said, 'It was okay, I got engaged.' 'Engaged!?' I blurted. 'Tell me all about it!' We had a great conversation about all of the details, the ring, who helped pulled it off and what made it so spectacular. What surprised me, however, was the fact that this employee almost didn't say anything and wouldn't have, had I not asked.

When leaders start to get to know you as a person and not the employee, you can find common ground, real meaningful conversations and improved performance. One example that demonstrates this is Aaron's story.

My brother Lucas was the Chief People Officer at a firm. He had a manager come to him and say, 'Aaron needs to go on a performance improvement plan for attendance.' Lucas asked more details; they pulled the reports and confirmed Aaron was consistently late for work. Lucas asked how conversations had gone about attendance and the manager said, 'Not great, he just sits there like he is in trouble and doesn't say much.'

I then encouraged Aaron's manager to sit down with Aaron and ask some questions that would encourage Aaron to be vulnerable. Long story short, Aaron was the youngest of seven children, and a bit of a 'whoops' baby (if you know what I mean). When he was born, his father was in a severe car accident, which made him highly medicated for nearly all of Aaron's life. The only thing in life that Aaron wanted was his father's approval. Since he felt he never had it, that projected to other figures of authority—including his work leaders. Aaron said he best responded to those who didn't see his flaws but the positive things he accomplishes.

By asking these probing questions, Lucas and the manager learned that if they could validate Adam, show him an increase of love first, and give a big stamp of approval on what he was doing well, he would be ready to take feedback. They then were able to talk through attendance issues and saw immediate improvement. Aaron moved from being on a performance improvement plan to being a top performer, and a year later, was promoted to a new role.

What changed? Aaron's leaders asked probing questions about *who* Aaron was, *what* made him tick and what *his needs* were. Having this conversation once was not enough. Aaron and all of us need continuous feedback and open, honest communication that advance the conversation about our job performance, alignment with company values and career goals.

Next time you have a one-on-one with a member of your team, don't focus on whether they 'exceed expectations', but have a genuine conversation from one human to another. Find out their current state in life, goals, desires, hopes and then correlate that conversation with how it aligns to the work they do for you each day. If you can get to that state of vulnerability with your employees, you'll start looking forward to one on one feedbacks instead of dreading having a performance management conversation.

Also, Lucas texted me saying Aaron is getting married in December 2022; and his dad will be there—I'm sure—with a big smile, being unbelievably proud of what his son is doing.

Ways You Can Re-Design Your Office To Make Your Workers Dance the Happy Dance

- Add mirrors to reflect the natural light you already get.
- Stimulate senses with a fresh scent—think oranges, lavender, vanilla—whatever you and your employees fancy.
- Use transparent or semi-transparent partitions instead of solid ones.
- Let your employees add their favourite colours to their desks through whatever means they want.
- Replace solid doors and cubicle walls with transparent or semi-transparent ones.
- Let your workers customize their desks—posters, plants, family photos, adorable cards from lovers or kids—anything they want. That way, they create their own little home within the office they always want to return to.
- Remove any huge objects that are blocking light from entering via the windows. You can move any obstructions to natural light, such as desks, bookshelves and filing cabinets.
- Productivity is frequently improved by the best ergonomic solutions. The workplace becomes extremely comfortable when jobs are designed to allow for good posture, less exertion, less motions and better heights and reaches. Provide comfortable cushions, ergonomic chairs and so on.
- Reorganize office space such that multiple employees (rather than just one executive) can sit in a windowed office.
- Don't underestimate the value of getting some fresh air by opening your windows.
- Adjust the office temperature. People work best when they're at a comfortable temperature. What's comfortable varies by person, but experts recommended working in air-conditioned office environments between 21 and 24 degrees Celsius.
- Create an office snack station to promote healthy eating.

Quick Hacks To Improve Employees' Well-Being (Because We're Living in the Era of Mental Health)

- Offer wellness classes (online or offline) on yoga, meditation, fitness or team-building. Even offering therapy sessions for those in need makes you an empathetic cutting-edge leader.
- Encourage your peers to develop best buddies at work.
- Let them listen to some nice music if that gets their mind relaxed during work.
- Offer flexible working hours, especially if your co-workers are drained or grieving.
- Take your team out for some good (healthy) food and celebrate even the smallest of wins.
- Chocolate makes life less hard. An appreciative sticky note with some nice chocolate at an employee's desk when they're stressed will flip their mood. Just trust me when I tell you that.
- Focus on their personal growth—nobody wants a dead-end job.
- Do you know that sitting for too long is the new smoking? Let your employees walk around and stretch their muscles—else, their brains will rot.
- Remind them to drink loads of water and get their 'beauty' sleep. It nourishes their minds and increases productivity in tremendous ways.
- Urge them to stay home if they're sick or mentally drained.
- Renovate your office to bring in some natural sunlight and add some good old greenery through plants.
- Let them know its *okay* to talk if they're *not* okay. The new-age leader values mental well-being over profits. Besides, if there's mental well-being, there *are* profits due to higher productivity. Simple logic.

Five Takeaways for You To Skim Through:

- Today's modern workplace is casual and fluid. Your workers don't have to suit up and bring leather briefcases to work. Your workers don't have to take appointments with your personal secretary to see you.

- A modern workplace culture attracts modern talent. If you tell young employees that you are up to date with today's values and trends, they'll be drawn towards you. That way, you create a team of the best talents across the world.

- The modern leader sees his company not as a money-making machine but as an organism with multiple living beings coming together to create new life and new magic. (Too poetic? My bad.)

- The modern leader cares about his peers' well-being, both mental and physical.

- The modern leader is not exploitative—he doesn't rule through fear. Rather, he motivates through rewards, praises and incentives.

10

WIDEN YOUR HORIZON; WIDEN YOUR LEADERSHIP

But, then, that's the point. In leadership, success is succession.[32]

—Andy Stanley

Think about a time in your life when you really were impacted by a great leader—someone who encouraged success, effort and productivity. What qualities did this leader possess? It's safe to say the leader you are thinking about, was more than just a figurehead with impressive technical skills. He or she was more likely to be someone who took interest in you, your work and your professional as well as personal growth.

The ability to develop the leadership potential of those on your team used to be a 'nice-to-have' skill in your arsenal. Today, it's *an absolute necessity*. While a traditional leader seeks to collect and wield authority, the new-age servant-leader seeks to share power, prioritizes the needs of others and assists others in becoming leaders.

As baby boomers retire from executive positions, millennials

---

[32]Andy Stanley, *Next Generation Leader*, Multnomah Books, 2003.

and Gen Z workers are expected to take over leadership roles and even transform organizations. There's often worry that companies are risking losing their best and brightest because they fail to transform workers into next-gen leaders. How can businesses attract and keep young talent while also teaching them management skills and providing them with the experience they need to become effective leaders? In order to create a process where millennials and Gen Z leaders can thrive, today's cutting-edge leader needs to create a more transparent leadership pipeline that enables youngsters to imagine themselves at the top, with the power to transform.

A study conducted by Deloitte recently showed that nearly 60 per cent of young professionals want to become leaders, yet *only 6 per cent* of companies feel their leadership pipeline is 'very ready'. Now, what does this lead to? You losing your star employees and champion performers because you failed to see they wanted to be like *you*—a leader!

The leader most people think about is someone who knows the job because he or she has done it themselves, but new-age leaders not only know the trade but also know their peers and teammates equally well. They have a sincere vested interest in others, care about what their co-workers need to do in their job and achieve career growth to become next-gen leaders themselves.

Imagine this: Manny is a high-potential, next-gen leader in your IT Department. Her annual salary is set at $65,000, with a $10,000 bonus possibility. You don't want to lose her raw talent to the competition; she's a coveted commodity on the job market. Manny, like the majority of millennials, is open to taking on a new role in order to expand her personal brand. You might lose anything from $15,000 to $30,000 in turnover charges if Manny leaves next year. Investing $1,500 to $2,000 in her personal and professional development, on the other hand, would undoubtedly keep her around for longer than planned. As a result, you'd come out ahead and have access to her skills and leadership abilities.

Companies were seeing the need to prepare their future leaders with the right skills for the changing future of work well before the Covid-19 outbreak. The pandemic has only underscored how critical it is for companies to consider how to develop the next generation of leaders. Why is it so vital to have a younger workforce? The fresh perspective, for one, says Bani Sodhi, who heads the International Future Leaders Program at the Adecco Group. 'Companies need to recognize the younger workforce is an asset,' Sodhi said. 'The fresh perspectives coming from the people who are experiencing world events at an earlier stage in their life adapt to the new at a faster pace and view the world from a different lens.'[33]

In a company with a cutting-edge, progressive culture of leadership, all employees, not just those with 'VP' or 'Chief' in their titles, are expected to think and act like leaders. You are not a leader—at most an ordinary manager—if you are content with people in your company coming to work every day, doing the same dull task for 5, 10, 15 years with no self-development.

What separates the good leaders from the great inspirational leaders is their ability to build a leadership culture that cultivates great leaders throughout their organization. Mike Myatt, the author of *Leadership Matters*, says that entrepreneurs shouldn't be 'in the business of creating followers, but of developing leaders'.

---

[33]'How Companies Can Prepare The Next Generation of Leaders', The Adecco Group, 15 July 2021, https://www.adeccogroup.com/future-of-work/latest-insights/how-companies-can-prepare-the-next-generation-of-leaders/, Accessed on 4 March 2022.

It should always be people over process because, when it's not, 'we'll continue to find ourselves in a crisis of leadership.'[34]

Most often, old-school leaders believe that employee happiness—and therefore, retention—is tied into gimmicky perks like company-wide happy hours or free office snacks, but it's *not*. Employees, especially your millennials and Gen Zers, want job security, health insurance and unlimited vacation. Additionally, they want professional development, and this progress is *your* responsibility as a modern leader.

You can't judge a great leader by their salary, or how many years of experience they have under their belt—that's only part of the picture and not even a telling one at that. If you want to identify a great leader, look no farther than their team. Taking on the job of cultivating internal talent is what distinguishes the excellent from the great. All leaders recognize the value of acquiring top talent, but it's what you do with that talent once they've formally joined your team that counts. Why is it so important to polish future leaders?

- **Employee loyalty**. Why would anyone want to leave you if you're investing in their growth?
- **Better delegation** and handling of crisis when you're not around. Your future leaders will ensure your company doesn't collapse just because you couldn't make it to work for a few days due to whatsoever reason.
- **Better management** of all tasks within and outside of the office. Your future leaders are great managers, remember?
- **Fantastic team-spirit, collaboration and communication**. Great minds think alike, remember? The more leaders you have, the stronger the team work is.

---

[34]Mike Myatt, *Leadership Matters,* Outskirts Press, 2007.

- Your **future leaders embrace change** and profit for it rather than running away from it. They basically adapt, like you.
- **Less recruitment costs.** If your loyal employees won't leave you because they're content, why would you have to hire more people, right?
- You ensure the **smooth succession of your company.**
- **More independence in your workers.** They won't scamper to you to make each and every petty decision. A confident workforce is an unbeatable workforce.
- **Better conflict-resolution** and solving of issues at all levels. Yes, you won't have to drain yourself out by playing mommy or daddy at all the levels of your company. You have too many other better things to do.

How Do You Spot Future Cutting-Edge Leaders?

- **They fix.** When you have an employee with that 'never give up' attitude, who looks for solutions and doesn't make excuses, you likely have a solid leadership candidate on your hands. When your team encounters a setback, look for the person who starts spouting possible plans of attack instead of moaning or groaning in defeat.
- **They shape-shift.** Top leaders invite the new and different. They are flexible and adapt quickly to changing business conditions. Jeff Bezos of Amazon is a prime (pun intended) example of this. He said in a commencement address, 'I didn't think I'd regret trying and failing. And I suspected I would always be haunted by a decision to not try at all.'
- **They're curious cats.** Most great ideas start with simple questions: 'What if I did this? Why does that happen?' Listen to employees' questions to spot those who are interested in

solving problems and learning more about how things work.

- **They're absolute experts in their field.** You can spot emerging leaders because they are sought out for advice on their subject knowledge. Leaders know how to use their knowledge, skills and personal characteristics to achieve exceptional results. Their leadership has been demonstrated through actions and activities over time—their work speaks for them, basically.

- **They are selfless.** Selfless leaders are quick to look inside to identify the causes of failure and quick to look outside to identify the causes of success. They listen first. They are humble, and they're human. Remember when Theo Epstein made us all fall in love and perfectly demonstrated in his humorous response to being named the world's greatest leader: 'Um, I can't even get my dog to stop peeing in the house!' Yes, that's a leader.

- **They are the *total* package.** You've heard these kinds of folks described in sports as 'multi-tool player', 'clutch hitter' or 'double/triple threat'.

  Now, I'm not a huge fan of sports analogies for corporate work; however, I do think I'm describing the same type of person. The total package for emerging leaders includes being a self-starter and having unlimited curiosity about people and businesses—someone that listens to understand and that can and will roll up their sleeves and dig in. The total package also includes passion—you can hear it in their voice and see it in their eyes.

- **They're well-liked by all.** Here's a different idea: inquire about your employees' opinions. Every now and again, poll all employees to see who, aside from themselves, they believe has the most leadership potential. Who would they trust to lead them into unknown territory? To whom would they most entrust their jobs or the company's future?

This bottom-up method to selecting leaders can pay off handsomely: you're not only showing your employees that you respect their input, but you're also recognizing people who employees already look to for advice.

- **They're great trainees.** Leadership candidates need to be coachable; learning isn't below their egos. The best leadership candidates aren't know-it-alls. Instead, they assess what they don't know objectively and seek out mentors, coaches and other advisors to help them catch up. They want for constructive criticism to aid in their learning and mastery of new skills.

- **They're thick-skinned.** They don't expect and don't want their life to be a cake-walk. The best leaders have grown up on the battle field. They've dealt with adversity, they've seen many tough situations and they approach challenges with confidence. They also know how to share, empathize and inspire. Nobody is born with these traits—they are absolutely learned skills. To identify future leaders, look for those with their chin up and an eye toward the horizon. Look for those that are preparing to go into battle. And most importantly, look for those that can get along with others through respect, positivity, empathy and inspiration.

- **And yes, they come in *all* shapes and sizes.** According to studies, those who talk the most in meetings (and who talk faster) are perceived to be more intelligent. Those individuals are likewise overwhelmingly male. (Wow, what a shock!)

    To put it another way, folks who appear to be in charge in a group situation may not actually be in charge at all—they're just talking a lot. Don't fall for it! Perhaps the finest leader is the one who can bring people together, or the silent individual who, while waiting to speak, comes up with the most innovative answer. Do you recall Chapter 3?

Furthermore, not all great leaders have the same leadership style. Some people are outgoing, while many others are more quiet and contemplative. Employees may take longer to trust an introverted leader but those ties can be far stronger. With personal projects, some leaders may be quite effective. Maybe they organize neighbourhood meetings or know how to raise funds for a project they care about. The point is, when it comes to finding the next kings and queens of your empire, don't make any distinctions.

How Does the Cutting-Edge Leader Create an Army of Cutting-Edge Leaders?

- **Cheer them on.** Whether it is punctuality, a good e-mail, a good way of handling conflict or a good habit, there are several reasons we can find to appreciate and acknowledge. Create an intention to appreciate something in someone in each conversation, no matter how small it is. Your small observation about someone can create a big impact in their minds and, of course, in your relationship with them. Acknowledgment and appreciation encourage positive behaviour. Acknowledge what you want to see more in your environment. The same happens with negative feedback. What we focus on grows.

- **Teach them to network.** When I started one of my first management positions, my boss constantly took me along to networking events, even though I absolutely dreaded them. But it was through such gatherings (in all their embarrassing splendour) that I learned how to form bonds with strangers, confidently initiate conversations and ask for what I need or want—while also delivering something mutually useful to my new acquaintance.

And because these are essential skills for leaders at all levels, it's critical to begin teaching your staff how to network effectively as soon as possible. You can begin small, even within your own company: Encourage your leaders-in-training to attend corporate activities (e.g., potlucks, sponsored lunches or after-work events) and, more significantly, to expand beyond chats with co-workers they already know.

As they gain confidence, you can engage them in community and professional activities, and eventually send them in to represent your firm in your place. They'll have essential contacts and the people skills needed to thrive when they advance into leadership roles.

- **Tell less, ask more.** You have to elicit answers out of your future gems. When someone comes to you for advice, try brainstorming with them by asking questions to allow them to think about their own ideas. Create a space for reflection. When people find their own answers, they are more committed and responsible for the same. At the same time, when you provide them the space to explore their own solutions, you move forward on trust and relationship with them.

- *Do not* **hover around them all the time.** I've realized that the best way to create leaders is to step back and let them manage themselves. Give people the tools they need, be there to answer questions and help, but ultimately, let them grow by not micromanaging their every move.

When an employee requires assistance with a task, he or she usually approaches you, and you can either take over or give the resources needed to complete the assignment. And, in most circumstances, carrying out that managerial responsibility is absolutely acceptable. When educating your staff to become leaders though, I've found that pushing them to figure out how to get what they need on their own is good. For example, if an employee needs assistance with a financial spreadsheet, instead of finishing it yourself, introduce your employee to the finance department's chief and let them do it.

Of course, this does not imply that you can—or should—do nothing to assist. But, little by little, let your employees take on more responsibility. Eventually, they'll learn how to get what they need even without your help.

- **Grant them growth.** To ensure your workers aren't stagnant in their positions (or worse, *leaving*), provide them with the right opportunities to grow so that they can one day pursue leadership roles within the company. Employees are an organization's most important asset, so invest in them.

  These opportunities for growth can include paying for formal education, internal or external training, bringing in industry professionals for lunch-and-learn programs—the options are endless. Supply employees with a calendar or list of upcoming professional development events, meetings of professional groups or associations and work-related events that they can attend on their own time.

- **Push them out of their comfort zone; give them bigger goals.** People who have mountains to climb tend to plan better, establish clear directions and push for the top. If all the tasks you give a person are ones that they are easily capable of achieving, they will have little reason to tap into their hidden leadership skills and seek new ways to accomplish higher goals.

- **Set an example.** Make a commitment to improve *your own* skills and competencies. If you're not continuously learning, why should your employees? Lead by example, and your team will follow. Demonstrate that you care about their accomplishment (who wouldn't?). Inquire about where they see their career going or how their role in the company is changing. These questions will make them think about their career and what they want to accomplish within the organization, even if they don't have a strategy in place now.

- **Invest in their formal training and courses.** For modern companies, it's normal to attract the attention of students worldwide and, in that way, gain access to a much larger pool of employees. This increases the chances to get your hands on the leadership material, but you need to be prepared to invest in some additional training and courses. In other words, only once your employees have received sufficient credentials will you have a better understanding of how to use and integrate their capabilities into your workforce, as well as how to further improve their skills through additional education. Don't limit this growth to their current role because leadership qualities aren't connected to a certain job title.

  There are courses through which they can learn to work within a case management framework—such as a course for counselling which will enable them to communicate effectively with co-workers and clients. Furthermore, this type of course goes beyond the theoretical and allows for a practical application of the curriculum material through work placement.

Five Takeaways for You To Skim Through:

- A mediocre and insecure leader is power-hungry and only wants followers; a great, cutting-edge leader creates other such leaders.
- Young leaders are the revolution—they're the transformers

and the future of the business world. The next-gen leader realizes that and invests in them.

- Leaders aren't naturally born, they're created. Most workers are leaders in some way or the other. The cutting-edge leader has a keen eye for such potential.

- Good communication, selflessness, composure, optimism and curiosity are signs of hardcore leadership potential. Keep your eyes open, your future leaders are all around you in the workplace.

- Coach them, tell them you see them as leaders, invest in their formal training, teach them to create business contacts and *do not* spoon-feed them. Let them solve their own issues under your guidance, and they're already transforming into leaders from mere employees.

11

MAN AND MACHINE
ARE BEST MATES

*The number one benefit of...technology is that it empowers
people to do what they want to do. It lets people be
creative. It lets people be productive. It lets people learn
things they didn't think they could learn before, and so in
a sense it is all about potential.*

—Steve Ballmer, American Businessman,
CEO of Microsoft (2000-2014)

Technology is now integrated into almost every part of our
jobs. We rely on computers for everything: Wi-Fi, email,
apps or our smartphones. Technology, on the other hand, is
continually evolving. Software and programmes are updated on
a regular basis, resulting in better versions of themselves. New
hardware is always outdating earlier laptop and desktop versions,
while new apps are being produced on a daily basis.

Leaders that embrace rapid technological shifts are more
likely to create a larger impact in the workplace. As the way
we learn and communicate continues to shift, so does the way
people lead teams. The most successful leaders at a worldwide
level are those who understood just how much technology can

aid them in managing people—helping them build teams and keeping track of work across all channels and in any location of the world.

The world as we know it now has undergone a dramatic transformation into the digital age; and, in order to stay up with the changes, businesses have placed a greater emphasis on digital transformation. Digital transition can be perplexing and frightening. Adaptation is easier though, if the leaders are confident in the changes and how they will benefit everyone. With their exceptional leadership qualities, leaders like Elon Musk, Bill Gates and Steve Jobs have embraced the digital transition and adapted to it extremely quickly. Microsoft, for example, reported a significant rise in earnings after switching to cloud computing. As a result, they have distinguished themselves as leaders. And with the advent of technology, they have upgraded their skills that go hand in hand with the changes necessary.

Technology has taken over everything as the world changes at a quick rate. In addition, technological advancement has flourished in the corporate sector. A technologically proficient leader understands the role that technology may play in a company's overall strategy. It is one of the most important qualities a leader should have.

Technologically capable leaders have a thorough understanding of the organization's strengths, products and services, as well as the capacity to resolve technical challenges and assist others in adapting to new advances. This ability will help you present yourself as a future leader who is well-versed in concepts and ideas and has exceptional problem-solving skills.

What Are the Benefits of Technology Colliding With Leadership?

- **You collaborate effectively.** Technology helps you to collaborate with your team in a variety of ways. Leadership necessitates communication, and you can easily interact and work with your team using apps like Skype, Dropbox, Evernote and even by email.

- **You are an influencer.** Technology does not mean only advanced computing and IT solutions—it also means social media and the new concept of social leadership. A leader now has the most wide-reaching channels of communication available. Through various social media platforms and blogs, they may influence their employees, encourage their sales teams, establish client loyalty and interact with peers. Mark Zuckerberg is a Facebook Inc. co-founder and serves as its chairman, CEO and controlling shareholder. He doesn't publish any tips on doing business but shares some family pics, news, events he has been to as a speaker, etc. All in all, he has millions of followers who don't expect anything from him but just want to keep an eye on the life of such an influential person of the twenty-first century. You are most likely to know Richard Branson as the founder of the Virgin Group. At present, there are over 400 brands under the Virgin brand. Branson's company, many years ago, was not hesitant to sign contracts with unknown bands (such as the Sex Pistols), and this led to Virgin's success. This British entrepreneur, billionaire, philanthropist and explorer is a terrific motivator as well as one of the world's wealthiest people. Motivational phrases, life situations and book recommendations abound Branson's Instagram account.

- **You save time and energy.** Using many programmes and

apps for the same function is one of the quickest ways to become less efficient and effective. When making your selection, keep in mind that each activity should only have one software or app associated with it. Stick with Evernote if you're using it for collaboration. Do not keep half of your documents in one location and the other half in another.

- **You lead anytime, anywhere.** Do you remember the old days when no important decision could be taken because the CEO or the manager in charge was away on a business trip and unreachable? Technology has made such scenes a thing of the past. By having software suites installed on all devices (desktop, laptop and mobile phones), directors and managers now have the ability to approve budgets, convene meetings and make decisions. From the luxury of a hotel room or the lounge of a business convention location, they may resolve any other crucial issues.

- **You can improve your company's culture.** The idea that digital transformation is primarily about technology is a myth. It's primarily about *people*—and improving their experiences as both employees and customers. For that reason, technology offers leaders a good excuse to reassess their organizational cultures—be it through online feedback forms or e-meetings.

- **Networking (I'm sure you've heard this word before.)** You frequently notice your online contact Martha posting intriguing articles, commenting and intelligently responding to online discussions when you visit Facebook. You're both interested in the same kinds of news and information, and you keep running into one other online. You don't pay attention at first. You quickly begin to know Martha's persona and aspirations. From afar, it's simple to get to know someone—their online presence, shares and comments speak for themselves. It becomes evident that you have similar interests, networks and philosophies. You begin to feel as though you know them even though you've never spoken to them one-on-one. The door to a more meaningful relationship has now opened. You might never take the relationship any further, but even so, Martha is in your head. If you, or anyone you know, ever has a need for the types of products, services or skills Martha has, she will be first on your list to call or recommend.

Perhaps networking seems to be an indulgence: like chatting when you could be achieving more important things. But effective networking marks the difference between strong leaders and merely good managers. It is also important to remember that *networking is work*. You can make great professional, personal, organizational and social progress by leading with good networking. Your networking helps you stay in touch with current trends, new knowledge, talent across the globe, find new partners/clients/ stakeholders/customers and promote your own brand. If modern business is war, online networking is your armour.

- Leaders know their network, first and foremost. You should have an idea of the types of people you want to have in your network. For example, if you sell makeup locally, you should connect with local women, or if you sell HR technology, you should connect with HR folks.
- Leaders choose a few associations with like-minded entrepreneurs and participate actively in discussions and events; they go to meetings as often as possible and work on one or two committees to leave their mark. Their goal is to basically be the first person everyone remembers and suggests when others ask, 'Do you know anyone who....'

- One of the best ways to network with people is to find common interests, so join something you are interested in. Just like with Mastermind groups, you can find and connect with your own hobby group through Facebook, Reddit and Meetup.

- Greeting old contacts is norm. E-leaders ask how projects they are working on are going, mention news articles they've seen about them and congratulate them on any recent successes they've had.

- Leaders skim through LinkedIn to find the best talent across the countries. Remember that the cutting-edge leader breaks barriers?

- Playing the slow game is usually their way to go. Just imagine—who would you rather reply to? The guy who goes, 'Hey! I saw your content and it was awesome, here's what stood out to me...' or the person who says, 'I like your content, do you have any opportunities for me?'

- New-age leaders create content, write articles on their areas of expertise and share relevant articles on social media platforms to let the world know what they're passionate about. That way, they build a brand, build trust and let people know they're up-to-date with today's happenings.

Tips for the E-Leader To Guide Their E-Team

- **Give Clear Instructions:** Simply telling somebody to do something is usually not the popular way to go about managing teams. Micro-managing isn't either which is why some managers avoid giving instructions with too many details. Based on my experience, it is better to provide more detailed descriptions of the tasks with examples of what the final result should look like. Give the team the freedom to execute it rather than less instructions and having to deal with potential misunderstandings.

- **Be There, Be Accessible:** It can be isolating working virtually. Don't make team members feel you are absent. Be in regular contact to talk not just about their day-to-day duties but beyond that to general queries about their day, mood and social life. Nobody listens to an invisible leader.
- **Choose the Right Tools:** Virtual teams don't have a physical location to meet and discuss every day, so creating a common meeting space online is vital to communication and collaboration. Sending a stream of emails to everyone on your virtual teams is not productive or efficient. Information gets lost, attachments get corrupted, inboxes fill up and your team members must remember to 'reply all' and read through long email threads to understand what's going on. There is a wealth of tools especially designed to facilitate collaboration and organize work with virtual teams. For example, Basecamp and Trello provide a place where remote employees can discuss a project, upload and share files, make comments, create to-do lists and more. Select the right tool for what your virtual teams need.
- **Face Your Team, *Literally*:** With Skype and email being available at everyone's fingertips, it is tempting to chat and send a quick email whenever there is something to discuss. This can easily lead to miscommunication. Video conversations, or at the very least, regular talks are more than a technique to avoid misunderstandings in virtual collaborations. They bring the team members closer together on a more intimate basis.
- **Choose Different Channels for Different Purposes:** Although it may seem counterintuitive, the experience taught us that multiple communication channels can contribute to a greater

efficiency of virtual teams. How come? Well, it turns out that every communication platform serves a different purpose. You cannot use an email to ask your employee about an urgent update. Similarly, you cannot videocall a teammate during dinner time for a small query; you'd rather send them a WhatsApp text and wait for their response whenever they're available. Email is great for official communication with strictly determined messages and clear goals. On the other side, live chat is much more convenient for everyday communication, while video conferencing suits complex discussions that require in-depth explanations.

- **Set a Slot for Small Talk:** Small talk may seem trivial, but it does big work for your teams' emotions. Even during the pandemic, a recent study by Rutgers University found small talk very beneficial toward employee's emotions. According to the study, morning office chit-chat can lead to increased energy, excitement and joy throughout the day.

  If you're having weekly virtual team meetings, leave time for employees to catch up and talk about their personal life. Encourage camera-shy employees to join or develop dedicated chat channels where they can discuss their favourite activities. Small talk can get out of hand, and before you know it, you're talking through every single TV show your co-workers are watching. Instead, set aside specific times for team-building tasks.

- **Be Aware of Different Time Zones:** If you're a global leader, you know your workforce is spread out across different continents. Never expect a California employee to be on a conference call at 8 a.m. EST—flexible hours will help everyone be more productive. Rotate meeting times every week to ensure that no one member is always getting up early for meetings and no one is returning home late.

- List all your team members on a paper.
- Add in their time zones.
- Add their clock-in and clock-out times you've gathered from their time tracking results.
- Find the ideal time slots for meetings through comparison.
- Once you've decided on the time, you can then handle remote meetings by holding Skype video conferences or through a communication system like Google hangouts.

- **Do a Small E-Party:** For example, after your team achieves a particular goal, organize a virtual reward ceremony. Send a small present to all team members and get everyone to open it at the same time during a video call. Online working doesn't have to be as bleak as most of us think it is.
- **Ask About Your Team's Progress:** You don't want to micromanage your team, but you'll still have to keep an eye on what they're doing and whether they're making the planned progress with their tasks.

- Glance at their time tracking reports.
- Establish and carry out regular daily meetings.
- Arrange occasional one-on-one meetings.
- Give consistent feedback via text, email or video calls about their work.

Management Tools Are Magical

You can handle your virtual projects easily through different e-tools. Using a number of management tools will greatly facilitate your project, task and team management—as well as ensure you save time by working on one document at the same time. All I can say is: God bless technology.

- **Project management tools** are great for keeping track of project progress 'from afar' and keeping an eye on deadlines.
- **Task management software** is great for defining and tracking tasks, as well as storing documents you need for work. ProofHub, Basecamp, Trello and Teamwork are some classic tools.
- **Team management tools** are great for facilitating collaboration among team members. For instance, Microsoft Teams, Google Meet, Zoom or Slack.
- **Screen sharing tools** are great when you need to help a team member set up a new program you'll both be using or anything else you need to perform from afar.
- **Online spreadsheets** are great when you have to work on documents simultaneously and have all changes saved and synced in real-time, automatically. Think Google Sheets, Zoho Sheet or Smartsheet.

Lastly, Create a Solid Virtual Team Culture

Admit it: your workers miss the face-to-face interaction with their co-workers, which a normal employee enjoys daily. And all this often makes these remote workers feel left out which is really bad. No one likes to be left alone, especially when you're part of a team. This is why you, as a leader, should encourage all your virtual employees to be a part of a virtual community. Such a virtual community would play a significant role in bridging the gap between the virtual team members. Also, make sure that this community is up 24/7 so that employees working from different time zones don't feel left out or isolated.

- Meet face-to-face from time to time, if possible. If you all live in the same country, you can organize get-togethers every couple of months. Organize a team dinner, go out bowling and get to know each other beyond your company titles.
- Try to establish virtual bonds. As you won't be able to throw pizza parties and play baseball together all that often, you can encourage people to strike online friendships. As a leader, you have to pave the way. Add your team members to LinkedIn and Twitter or even Facebook.
- Make all the meetings remote-friendly. Sometimes, only part of the team is virtual, and the non-virtual part of the team may be tempted to hold separate meetings. To avoid the remote crowd feeling left out, establish the practice of holding all meetings, even the quick ones, online.

Five Takeaways for You To Skim Through:

- Technology can help you lead your team in the most effective and efficient ways—you save time and money through different apps and tools.
- The cutting-edge leader creates a widespread online presence through networking. Your network is your net worth.
- The cutting-edge leader is also an influencer. He creates influence by showing his knowledge, skills, experience and passion online.
- The cutting-edge leader finds the best pool of talent online. His X-Men come from all around the world—in a digital, barrier-less world.
- The cutting-edge leader leads his virtual teams like a boss— he/she creates a culture of virtual teams in his organization by

ensuring one-on-one online meets, virtual group discussions and creating groups on Facebook, LinkedIn and Instagram such that his/her team can interact more.